BREAKING THE CHAINS

OF

ABUSIVE RELATIONSHIP

A Blueprint to Freedom from Captivity

Reclaiming Your Life Back!

Justin J. Williams

Table of Contents

Introduction

In the silence of suffering, behind closed doors, countless individuals grapple with the unseen shackles of abusive relationships. This book is a guiding light for those who find themselves caught in the intricate web of manipulation, control, and emotional turmoil. "Breaking the Chains of Abusive Relationships" is not just a narrative; it's a lifeline for those seeking liberation.

Every story of empowerment begins with the courage to recognize the signs. As we embark on this transformative journey, we'll navigate the nuances of emotional abuse, unveil the veiled manipulations, and understand the cyclical patterns that keep us captive. Together, we'll spot the red flags that, when heeded, become the first steps toward breaking free.

But breaking free isn't just about escaping; it's about finding the strength to speak, to share, and to shatter the silence that veils the pain. In this journey, we'll explore the power of breaking that silence and overcoming the fear and shame that bind us to our struggles. We'll discover the importance of building a support system, seeking professional help, and crafting a safety plan that paves the way to a brighter future.

This book is a roadmap to taking back control—setting boundaries, honing assertiveness, and cultivating self-esteem. It's a testament to the resilience within, helping you manage anger, empower yourself, and ultimately regain the reins of your life.

Leaving an abusive relationship is a profound step, and we'll navigate this process meticulously. We'll understand the significance of leaving, plan exit strategies, explore legal protections, and ensure a safe departure. The journey doesn't end here; it evolves into healing and recovery.

As we delve into the realms of processing trauma, rebuilding trust, and embracing self-care, we'll witness the metamorphosis from survivor to thriver. Moving forward, setting goals, building healthy relationships, and finding joy become not just aspirations but achievable milestones.

Yet, the journey is not solitary. This book is a call to action, urging you to support others, recognize signs in those around you, and become an advocate for change. Together, we'll break the cycle, preventing abuse in future relationships, teaching healthy relationship skills, and fostering a culture of non-violence.

Join me in this exploration of strength, resilience, and the unwavering human spirit. Let this be your guide, your ally, and your beacon as we embark on the path to breaking the chains of abusive relationships.

Chapter 1: Recognizing the Signs

Understanding Emotional Abuse

Emotional abuse is a form of abuse that can be just as damaging as physical abuse, yet it often goes unnoticed and unaddressed. It is a pattern of behavior that aims to control, manipulate, and demean the victim, leaving them feeling powerless and trapped. Unlike physical abuse, emotional abuse does not leave visible scars, making it harder to recognize and address. In this section, we will delve deeper into understanding emotional abuse, its effects, and how to identify it in a relationship.

What is Emotional Abuse?

Emotional abuse is a systematic pattern of behavior that undermines an individual's self-worth, confidence, and emotional well-being. It involves manipulating, intimidation, and control tactics to gain power over the victim. Emotional abusers often employ various tactics such as gaslighting, belittling, humiliation, isolation, and constant criticism to erode the victim's self-esteem and independence.

The Effects of Emotional Abuse

The effects of emotional abuse can be long-lasting and devastating. Victims of emotional abuse often experience a range of emotional, psychological, and physical symptoms. They may suffer from low self-esteem, anxiety, depression, and a constant sense of fear and worthlessness. The constant criticism and belittlement can lead to feelings of shame, guilt, and self-blame. Over time, the victim may lose their sense of identity and become isolated from friends and family, as the abuser seeks to control and manipulate their social interactions.

Signs of Emotional Abuse

Since emotional abuse frequently happens gradually and covertly, recognizing it might be difficult. Some common signs can help identify an emotionally abusive relationship. These signs include:

Constant criticism and belittlement: The abuser consistently puts down the victim, criticizes their appearance, abilities, or decisions, and undermines their self-confidence.

Gaslighting: Gaslighting is a manipulative tactic where the abuser distorts the victim's perception of reality, making them doubt their memory, judgment, and sanity.

Isolation: The abuser seeks to isolate the victim from friends, family, and support networks, making them dependent on the abuser for emotional support and validation.

Control and manipulation: Emotional abusers exert control over every aspect of the victim's life, making decisions for them, monitoring their activities, and restricting their freedom.

Intense jealousy and possessiveness: The abuser displays extreme jealousy, constantly questioning the victim's loyalty and accusing them of infidelity without any evidence.

Emotional blackmail: The abuser uses guilt, threats, or manipulation to get what they want from the victim, often making them feel responsible for the abuser's emotions and actions.

Lack of empathy: The abuser shows a consistent lack of empathy towards the victim's feelings and needs, dismissing their emotions and minimizing their experiences.

Understanding the Dynamics of Emotional Abuse

Emotional abuse often follows a cycle, which can make it even more difficult for the victim to recognize and leave the abusive relationship. Typically, the cycle comprises three phases:

Tension-building phase: During this phase, tension and conflict start to escalate. The victim could experience anxiety about upsetting the abuser because they anticipate their rage or outbursts.

Explosion phase: In this phase, the tension reaches its peak, and the abuser may engage in verbal or emotional attacks. The victim may experience intense fear, anxiety, and emotional distress.

Honeymoon phase: After the explosion phase, the abuser may apologize, show remorse, and promise to change. They could show the victim a lot of love, give them gifts, and make promises about a brighter future. This phase can create a false sense of hope and make it harder for the victim to leave the relationship.

Understanding the dynamics of the abuse cycle is crucial in recognizing the patterns and breaking free from the cycle of abuse.

Identifying Manipulative Behaviors

The first step in leaving an unhealthy, and abusive relationship is identifying and comprehending any potential manipulative actions. Manipulation is a tactic used by abusers to gain control and power over their victims. By identifying these behaviors, you can begin to regain your autonomy and take steps toward breaking free from the chains of abuse.

Gaslighting

Gaslighting is a common manipulative behavior used by abusers to make their victims doubt their reality. The abuser may deny their conduct, twist the facts, or cause the victim to doubt their recall or sanity. Gaslighting can be subtle, making it difficult to recognize at first. The abuser may constantly contradict the victim, dismiss their feelings, or blame them for the abuse. Over time, the victim may start to question their perception of reality, leading to feelings of confusion, self-doubt, and a loss of confidence.

Isolation

Isolation is another manipulative tactic used by abusers to control their victims. They may gradually cut off the victim from their friends, family, and support systems, making them dependent solely on the abuser for emotional and social support. The victim may feel confined and alone if the abuser forbids or discourages them from participating in activities outside of the relationship. The abuser obtains greater power and makes it more difficult for the victim to get assistance or leave the abusive environment when they isolate themselves.

Blame-Shifting

Abusers often engage in blame-shifting as a way to avoid taking responsibility for their actions. They may shift the blame onto the victim, making them feel guilty or responsible for the abuse. The abuser may use phrases like "You made me do it" or "If you hadn't done that, I wouldn't have reacted this way." By placing the blame on the victim, the abuser manipulates them into believing that they are the cause of the abuse, further eroding their self-esteem and self-worth.

Manipulative Language

Abusers are skilled at using manipulative language to control and manipulate their victims. They may use tactics such as belittling, name-calling, or using sarcasm to demean and degrade the victim. They may also use threats, ultimatums, or coercion to get their way. Manipulative language is designed to make the victim feel powerless and submissive, further reinforcing the abuser's control over them.

Love-Bombing

Love-bombing is a manipulative behavior where the abuser showers the victim with excessive affection, attention, and gifts to gain their trust and loyalty. This behavior is often used in the early stages of a relationship to create a sense of dependency and attachment. The abuser may make grand gestures, constantly praise the victim, and make them feel like they are the center of their world. Once the victim is emotionally invested, the abuser may gradually withdraw their affection and become more controlling and abusive.

Financial Control

Financial control is a manipulative tactic used by abusers to maintain power and control over their victims. They may control the victim's access to money, limit their financial independence, or prevent them from working or pursuing their career. By controlling the finances, the abuser can make the victim dependent on them for their basic needs, making it harder for the victim to leave the abusive relationship.

Emotional Manipulation

Emotional manipulation is a pervasive tactic used by abusers to exploit the emotions and vulnerabilities of their victims. They may use guilt, fear, or pity to manipulate the victim into doing what they want. Emotional manipulation can take many forms, such as playing the victim, using emotional blackmail, or withholding affection as a form of punishment.

By manipulating the victim's emotions, the abuser maintains control and power over them.

Intimidation and Threats

Threats and intimidation are common tools used by abusers to keep their victims under control and engender dread. They may use physical violence, aggressive gestures, or destroy property to intimidate the victim. They might threaten to hurt the victim, their family members, or even themselves if they try to leave or ask for assistance. Intimidation and threats create a climate of fear and make it difficult for the victim to assert their independence or challenge the abuser's control.

Recognizing these manipulative behaviors is the first step towards breaking free from an abusive relationship. By understanding the tactics used by abusers, you can begin to reclaim your power and take the necessary steps to break the chains of abuse. You are not alone, and there is help available to support you on your journey to freedom and healing.

Recognizing the Cycle of Abuse

To break free from an abusive relationship, it is crucial to understand the cycle of abuse. Abuse is not a one-time event but rather a pattern of behavior that repeats itself over time. Three phases usually make up this cycle: the growing tension phase, the explosion phase, and the honeymoon period. By recognizing these patterns, you can gain insight into the dynamics of the relationship and take steps toward breaking free.

The Tension-Building Phase

The phase of tension-building is the initial stage of the abuse cycle. During this phase, the abuser may become increasingly irritable, critical, and controlling. Small arguments and conflicts may escalate, and the victim may feel a sense of walking on eggshells, constantly trying to avoid triggering the abuser's anger. The tension in the relationship steadily increases, creating a sense of fear and anxiety for the victim.

In this phase, the victim may try to appease the abuser, believing that their actions can prevent the abuse from occurring. They may become overly compliant, sacrificing their own needs and desires to keep the peace. Despite their efforts, the tension continues to build, leading to the next phase of the cycle.

The Explosion Phase

The explosion phase is characterized by a sudden and intense outburst of abuse. This can take various forms, including physical, emotional, verbal, or sexual abuse. The abuser may unleash their anger and frustration on the victim, using intimidation, threats, or violence to exert control and power. The victim may feel helpless, trapped, and terrified during this phase.

The explosion phase is often the most dangerous and traumatic part of the cycle. The abuse can cause physical injuries, emotional scars, and long-lasting trauma.

The Honeymoon Phase

Following the explosion phase, the cycle enters the honeymoon phase. During this phase, the abuser may display remorse, apologize, and promise change. They may shower the victim with affection, gifts, and attention, creating a false sense of security and hope for a better future. The abuser may blame external factors or stressors for their behavior, making excuses for their actions.

The honeymoon phase can be confusing and conflicting for the victim. They could have a strong desire to think that the abuser has changed and that they can still save the relationship. This phase often leads to feelings of hope and optimism, making it difficult for the victim to leave the relationship.

The Cycle Repeats

The tension-building phase of the abuse cycle begins when the honeymoon phase concludes. The pattern repeats itself, with the tension gradually increasing, leading to another explosion of abuse, followed by a brief period of remorse and reconciliation. This cycle can continue indefinitely unless intervention occurs.

It is important to understand that the cycle of abuse is not static and can vary in duration and intensity. Some relationships may have shorter cycles, while others may have longer ones. The length of each phase can also vary. The overall pattern remains the same.

One of the most important steps in leaving an abusive relationship is realizing the abuse cycle. By understanding the predictable patterns, you can begin to see the reality of the situation and the need for change.

Spotting Red Flags

Being able to spot the warning signs of possible abuse is essential if we want to prevent ourselves from getting into an abusive relationship. While every relationship is unique, certain warning signs commonly appear in abusive dynamics. By being aware of these red flags, we can empower ourselves to make informed decisions and avoid falling into harmful relationships.

Early Warning Signs

Controlling Behavior: One of the earliest red flags in an abusive relationship is when your partner exhibits controlling behavior. This can manifest in various ways, such as constantly checking your phone or social media accounts, dictating who you can spend time with, or making decisions on your behalf without your input.

Jealousy and Possessiveness: Excessive jealousy and possessiveness are warning signs of an unhealthy relationship. Excessive jealousy or attempts to distance you from friends and family could be warning signs of abuse in the future from your partner.

Quick Involvement: While it is normal to feel a strong connection with someone early on in a relationship, it is important to be cautious if your partner wants to rush the relationship or declares their love too quickly. This could be a tactic to gain control over you and manipulate your emotions.

Isolation: Abusers often try to isolate their victims from their support systems. It is a red flag of possible abuse when your partner tries to shut off communication or prevents you from seeing friends and family.

Blaming Others: Pay attention to how your partner talks about their past relationships. If they consistently blame their exes for all the problems in their previous relationships, it could be an indication that they have difficulty taking responsibility for their actions.

Emotional and Verbal Abuse

Constant Criticism: If your partner constantly criticizes you, belittles your achievements, or undermines your self-esteem, it is a form of emotional abuse. This behavior is meant to erode your confidence and make you dependent on them.

Name-Calling and Insults: Verbal abuse often involves name-calling, insults, and derogatory language. It is a blatant sign of an abusive relationship if your spouse speaks poorly of you frequently.

Gaslighting: Gaslighting is a manipulative tactic used by abusers to make their victims doubt their reality. They may deny or distort events, make you question your memory, or make you feel like you are going crazy. If you find yourself constantly questioning your perception of reality, it is a sign of gaslighting.

Threats and Intimidation: Any form of threats or intimidation, whether it is physical or emotional, is a major red flag. If your partner uses fear to control you or makes you feel unsafe, it is important to take these warning signs seriously.

Physical Abuse

Physical Aggression: Physical abuse is a clear indication of an abusive relationship. It's important to get assistance and leave the situation as soon as your partner starts acting physically aggressively toward you, such as shoving, slapping, or hitting.

Destroying Property: Damaging or destroying your personal belongings is another form of physical abuse. It is a way for the abuser to exert control and instill fear in you.

Forced Sexual Acts: Any form of non-consensual sexual activity is a serious violation and a clear sign of abuse. If your partner forces you into sexual acts against your will, it is important to reach out for support and seek help.

Manipulative Tactics

Love-Bombing: Love-bombing is a manipulative tactic used by abusers to overwhelm their victims with excessive affection and attention. While it may initially feel flattering, it is often a way to manipulate and control you.

Guilt-Tripping: Abusers often use guilt as a means of control. They may make you feel guilty for their actions or manipulate you into thinking that you are responsible for their behavior.

Minimizing and Denying: When confronted about their abusive behavior, abusers often minimize or deny their actions. They may downplay the severity of their behavior or shift the blame onto you.

Financial Control: Another red flag is when your partner exerts control over your finances. This can include limiting your access to money, controlling your spending, or preventing you from working.

It is important to remember that these red flags are not definitive proof of an abusive relationship, but they serve as warning signs that should not be ignored. If you notice any of these behaviors in your relationship, it is crucial to seek support from trusted friends, family, or professionals who can help you navigate the situation safely.

Chapter 2: Breaking the Silence

Overcoming Fear and Shame

Fear and shame are two powerful emotions that often keep individuals trapped in abusive relationships. These emotions can be paralyzing, making it difficult for victims to seek help or take steps toward breaking free from the cycle of abuse.

Understanding Fear

Fear is a natural response to danger or threat, and in an abusive relationship, fear becomes a constant companion. A victim's dread of retaliation, physical damage, or even just uncertainty might keep them stuck in an abusive cycle. It is important to recognize that fear is a normal response to an abnormal situation. The first step in conquering this fear is realizing and accepting it.

Challenging Shame

Shame is another powerful emotion that often accompanies abuse. Victims may feel ashamed of their situation, blaming themselves for the abuse they endure. It is crucial to understand that the shame lies with the abuser, not the victim. No one deserves to be mistreated or abused, and it is important to challenge and reject any feelings of shame that may arise.

Building Self-Esteem

One of the most effective ways to overcome fear and shame is by building self-esteem. Abusers often manipulate their victims into believing that they are worthless, and undeserving of love and respect. By working on building self-esteem, individuals can regain their sense of self-worth and recognize their strength and resilience.

Several strategies can help in building self-esteem:

Positive affirmations: Practice positive self-talk and affirmations to counteract the negative messages that have been internalized. Repeat affirmations like "I deserve to be treated with kindness" or "I deserve love and respect" several times.

Celebrate achievements: Recognize and celebrate even the smallest achievements. This could be as simple as completing a task or standing up for oneself. By acknowledging these accomplishments, individuals can boost their self-confidence.

Surround yourself with positive influences: Seek out supportive and positive people who can provide encouragement and validation. Surrounding oneself with individuals who believe in their worth can help victims rebuild their self-esteem.

Engage in self-care: Make self-care activities that support your emotional, mental, and physical health a priority. This could include exercise, meditation, journaling, or engaging in hobbies that bring joy and fulfillment.

Educating Yourself

Knowledge is power, and educating yourself about abuse can help dispel fear and shame. Understanding the dynamics of abusive relationships, the tactics used by abusers, and the resources available can empower individuals to make informed decisions and take steps toward breaking free.

There are several ways to educate yourself about abuse:

Read books and articles: There are numerous books and articles available that provide valuable insights into abusive relationships, the effects of abuse, and strategies for healing and recovery. Gaining knowledge about abuse might assist you in realizing that there is hope for a better future and that you are not alone.

Attend support groups: Joining support groups or attending workshops can provide a safe space to share experiences, gain support from others who have been through similar situations, and learn from their journeys toward healing and empowerment.

Seek professional help: Consider reaching out to therapists or counselors who specialize in working with survivors of abuse. They can provide guidance, support, and tools to help you overcome fear and shame.

Taking Small Steps

Overcoming fear and shame is a process that takes time and patience. It is important to remember that healing and breaking free from an abusive relationship is a journey, and it is okay to take small steps toward change.

Here are a few quick actions you can do:

Speak with a family member or someone you can trust: Feeling less alone and receiving emotional support might be obtained by confiding in a trusted person about your experience. They can also offer guidance and help you explore your options.

Create a safety plan: Developing a safety plan can help you feel more in control and prepared for any potential risks or challenges that may arise. This plan may include identifying safe places to go, important phone numbers, and steps to take in case of an emergency.

Seek legal advice: If you are considering leaving the relationship, it may be helpful to consult with a lawyer who specializes in domestic violence cases. They can guide legal options and help you understand your rights.

Overcoming fear and shame is a process that requires patience, self-compassion, and support. By taking small steps toward breaking free from an abusive relationship, you can reclaim your life and build a future filled with safety, happiness, and empowerment.

Building a Support System

Creating a network of support is essential if you are in an abusive relationship. It can provide you with the strength, encouragement, and resources you need to break free from the chains of abuse.

Understanding the Importance of Support

Feeling alone and isolated is a common experience for those who are stuck in abusive relationships. It can be challenging to ask for assistance since the abuser frequently manipulates and controls your interactions with other people. Building a support system is essential for your well-being and your journey towards breaking free.

Having a support system can provide you with emotional support, validation, and a safe space to share your experiences. It can help you gain perspective, reinforce your self-worth, and remind you that you are not alone. A support system can offer practical assistance, such as helping you find resources, providing a place to stay, or assisting with legal matters.

Identifying Supportive Individuals

When building a support system, it is important to identify individuals who are trustworthy, understanding, and non-judgmental. These individuals can be friends, family members, colleagues, or professionals who specialize in domestic violence. The following characteristics of encouraging people should be sought after:

Empathy: Seek out individuals who can empathize with your situation and validate your feelings. They should be able to understand the complexities of abuse and provide a listening ear without judgment.

Trustworthiness: Choose people who can be trusted to keep your experiences confidential. Confidentiality is crucial, especially if you are still in the relationship and fear retaliation from your abuser.

Non-judgmental: Surround yourself with people who will not blame you for the abuse or question your decisions. They should respect your autonomy and support you in whatever choices you make.

Knowledgeable: Consider seeking support from professionals who have experience in dealing with domestic violence. They can provide you with valuable guidance, resources, and referrals to other support services.

Building a Support Network

Once you have identified supportive individuals, it is important to build a network of people who can provide different types of support. Here are some key roles that can be filled by different individuals in your support system:

Emotional Support: These individuals are there to listen, validate your experiences, and provide emotional comfort.

They can be friends, family members, or support group members who have gone through similar situations.

Practical Support: These individuals can offer practical assistance, such as helping you find a safe place to stay, providing transportation, or helping with childcare. They can be friends, family members, or community organizations.

Professional Support: Seek out professionals who specialize in domestic violence, such as therapists, counselors, or advocates. They can provide you with guidance, safety planning, and access to resources.

Legal Support: If you are considering legal action or need assistance with legal matters, consult with an attorney who specializes in domestic violence cases. They can help you understand your rights, obtain protective orders, and navigate the legal system.

Communicating Your Needs

Building a support system requires effective communication. It is important to communicate your needs and boundaries to the individuals in your support network. The following advice can help you communicate effectively:

Be honest: Share your experiences and feelings openly with your support system. Honesty is crucial for them to understand your situation and provide appropriate support.

Set boundaries: Communicate your boundaries and expectations. Let your support system know what you need from them and what you are comfortable with.

Ask for help: Never be afraid to ask for assistance when you need it. Your support system is there to assist you, so reach out when you need support, advice, or practical assistance.

Be open to feedback: Your support system may offer suggestions or advice based on their own experiences or expertise. Be open to their feedback, but remember that you have the final say in your decisions.

Maintaining and Expanding Your Support System

Building a support system is an ongoing process. It is important to maintain and nurture the relationships within your support network. Here are some tips for maintaining and expanding your support system:

Express gratitude: Express gratitude for the help you've been given. Expressing gratitude can strengthen your relationships and encourage continued support.

Attend support groups: Consider joining support groups for survivors of abuse. These groups offer a secure setting for people to talk about their experiences, get support, and gain knowledge from others who have been in similar circumstances.

Seek professional help: Continue seeking therapy or counseling to address the emotional and psychological impact of the abuse. A professional can help you navigate the healing process and provide ongoing support.

Connect with community resources: Research local organizations that provide support for survivors of abuse. These organizations often offer counseling, legal assistance, and other resources that can further strengthen your support system.

Building a support system takes time and effort. Regaining your life and leaving an abusive relationship requires taking this important step. Surround yourself with individuals who believe in your strength and resilience, and never hesitate to reach out for help when you need it.

Seeking Professional Help

Seeking professional help is a crucial step in breaking free from an abusive relationship. While it may be difficult to reach out for assistance, professional support can provide you with the guidance, resources, and tools necessary to navigate the complexities of leaving an abusive partner and rebuilding your life.

The Importance of Professional Help

When you are in an abusive relationship, it is common to feel isolated, trapped, and overwhelmed. Seeking professional help can offer you a safe space to share your experiences, emotions, and concerns without judgment. A trained professional, such as a therapist or counselor, can provide you with the necessary support and guidance to help you understand the dynamics of abuse, identify your options, and develop a plan for your safety and well-being.

Professional help is essential for several reasons:

Validation and Empowerment

One of the most significant benefits of seeking professional help is the validation and empowerment it provides. You can realize that you deserve to live a life free from violence and control and that the abuse is not your fault with the assistance of a professional. They can help you regain your self-esteem, confidence, and sense of self-worth, which may have been eroded by the abusive relationship.

Safety Planning

A professional can assist you in creating a safety plan tailored to your specific situation. This plan's activities are intended to safeguard your physical and emotional health both before and after you leave the abusive relationship. They can help you identify potential risks, develop strategies to minimize harm and connect you with resources such as shelters, hotlines, and legal services.

Emotional Support

It can be extremely difficult and daunting to leave an abusive relationship. A professional can provide you with a safe and supportive environment to express your feelings, process your trauma, and work through the complex emotions associated with leaving an abusive partner. They can help you develop coping mechanisms and provide you with tools to manage anxiety, depression, and other mental health issues that may arise as a result of the abuse.

Education and Awareness

A professional can educate you about the dynamics of abuse, helping you understand the patterns and behaviors that are characteristic of an abusive relationship. This knowledge is crucial in breaking the cycle of abuse and preventing future abusive relationships. They can also provide you with information about your legal rights, resources available in your community, and support groups where you can connect with others who have experienced similar situations.

Types of Professionals to Seek Help From

When seeking professional help, it is important to find a qualified and experienced professional who specializes in domestic violence and trauma. Here are some types of professionals you may consider reaching out to:

Therapist or Counselor

A therapist or counselor who specializes in domestic violence can provide you with individual therapy to address the emotional and psychological impact of the abuse. They can help you process your trauma, develop coping strategies, and work towards healing and recovery.

Domestic Violence Advocate

Domestic violence advocates are professionals who are trained to support survivors of abuse. They can provide you with information, resources, and advocacy services. They can help you navigate the legal system, connect you with shelters and support groups, and assist you in accessing community resources.

Support Group Facilitator

Support groups offer a safe and supportive environment for survivors of abuse to share their experiences, learn from others, and gain support. Support group facilitators are trained professionals who can guide group discussions, provide resources, and offer emotional support.

Legal Professional

If you are considering legal action, consulting with a lawyer who specializes in domestic violence can be beneficial. They can provide you with legal advice, help you understand your rights, and assist you in obtaining protective orders or filing for divorce or custody.

Overcoming Barriers to Seeking Help

Seeking professional help can be challenging due to various barriers that survivors of abuse may face. It is important to acknowledge and address these barriers to ensure you receive the support you need:

Fear and Shame

Fear and shame are common emotions experienced by survivors of abuse. It is essential to remember that the abuse is not your fault, and seeking help is a courageous step towards reclaiming your life. Professional help can provide you with the tools and support to overcome these emotions and move toward healing.

Financial Constraints

Financial constraints can make it difficult to access professional help. However, many organizations and agencies offer free or low-cost services for survivors of abuse. Reach out to local domestic violence shelters, community centers, or helplines to inquire about available resources.

Lack of Awareness

Some survivors may not be aware of the resources and support available to them. Educate yourself about domestic violence organizations, helplines, and support groups in your area. Reach out to these organizations for information and guidance.

Cultural and Language Barriers

Cultural and language barriers can make it challenging for survivors to seek help. Look for professionals who are culturally competent and can provide services in your preferred language. Many organizations have interpreters or bilingual staff members who can assist you.

Seeking professional help is a vital step in breaking free from an abusive relationship. It provides you with the support, guidance, and resources necessary to navigate the challenges of leaving and recovering from abuse. Reach out and take the first step towards reclaiming your life and breaking the chains of abuse.

Creating a Safety Plan

You are in an abusive relationship; it is crucial to prioritize your safety above all else. Making a safety plan will help you deal with the unknowns and difficulties that come with ending an abusive relationship. A safety plan is a personalized strategy that outlines steps you can take to protect yourself and minimize the risk of harm.

Assessing Your Risk

Before you can create an effective safety plan, it is important to assess the level of risk you face in your abusive relationship. Understanding the potential dangers can help you develop strategies to mitigate them. Consider the following factors when evaluating your risk:

History of violence: Reflect on the frequency and severity of past incidents of abuse. Has the violence escalated over time? Has a weapon ever been used to threaten you?

Threats: Take note of any threats made by your abusive partner, whether they are directed towards you, your children, or your loved ones. Harmful threats must be treated very seriously.

Access to weapons: Determine if your partner has access to firearms or other dangerous weapons. If so, this increases the risk of severe harm.

Isolation: Assess the level of isolation imposed by your partner. Are you cut off from friends, family, or support networks? Seeking assistance or leaving an abusive relationship may be more difficult when one is isolated.

Substance abuse: If your partner abuses drugs or alcohol, it can further escalate the risk of violence and unpredictable behavior.

Control tactics: Think about your abusive partner's methods of control. Do they monitor your activities, control your finances, or restrict your access to transportation?

By evaluating these factors, you can gain a clearer understanding of the risks involved and tailor your safety plan accordingly.

Identifying Safe Spaces

When creating a safety plan, it is essential to identify safe spaces where you can seek refuge in times of crisis. These safe spaces should be locations where your abusive partner cannot easily find or access you. Consider the following options:

Safe homes: Identify friends, family members, or trusted individuals who can provide you with a safe place to stay temporarily. Ensure that these individuals are aware of your situation and willing to support you.

Domestic violence shelters: Research local domestic violence shelters in your area. These shelters offer confidential and secure accommodations for individuals fleeing abusive relationships. They can also provide additional resources and support.

Public spaces: Identify public spaces where you can go to seek safety, such as libraries, community centers, or places of worship. These spaces can provide temporary refuge during times of crisis.

Workplace: If your workplace is a safe environment, inform your supervisor or human resources department about your situation. They can help implement safety measures and support you during this challenging time.

Keep the locations of your safe spaces confidential and share them only with trusted individuals who can assist you in an emergency.

Communication and Documentation

Maintaining open lines of communication and documenting incidents of abuse are crucial aspects of creating a safety plan. These steps can help you gather evidence, seek support, and ensure your safety. Consider the following:

Emergency contacts: Compile a list of emergency contacts, including local law enforcement, domestic violence hotlines, and trusted friends or family members. In the event of an emergency, keep this list close at hand.

Code words: Establish a code word or phrase with trusted individuals that can indicate when you are in immediate danger or need assistance. This can help you communicate discreetly without alerting your abusive partner.

Documenting abuse: Keep a record of incidents of abuse, including dates, times, and descriptions of what occurred. Take photos of any visible injuries or property damage. If you choose to ask for legal protection or cooperate with law authorities, these documents may be helpful.

Secure communication: If possible, use secure communication methods when reaching out for help or discussing your situation. This can include encrypted messaging apps or private browsing modes on your devices.

Safety Measures at Home

Creating a safe environment within your home is essential for your well-being. Implementing safety measures can help protect you and your children from harm. Consider the following steps:

Secure important documents: Gather and secure important documents such as identification papers, passports, birth certificates, financial records, and any legal documents related to your relationship. Keep them in a safe place outside of your home, such as a trusted friend's house or a safe deposit box.

Change locks and passwords: To stop your violent partner from entering your house, if at all possible, replace the locks on your windows and doors. Change passwords for your online accounts to maintain privacy and security.

Safety devices: Install security measures in your home, such as a security system, motion sensor lights, or window and door alarms. By taking these steps, you can feel more secure and dissuade an abusive partner.

Escape routes: Identify and plan escape routes within your home. Determine the quickest and safest way to exit each room, and practice these routes with your children if applicable.

Emergency bag: Prepare an emergency bag containing essential items such as clothing, toiletries, medications, important documents, and a small amount of cash. Keep this bag in a discreet location where you can easily access it if you need to leave quickly.

Creating a safety plan is an ongoing process. Regularly review and update your plan as needed to ensure it remains effective and relevant to your circumstances. Seek support from professionals, such as domestic violence advocates or counselors, who can provide guidance and assistance throughout this journey. Your safety and well-being are paramount, and by taking proactive steps, you can break free from the chains of abuse and create a brighter future for yourself.

Chapter 3: Taking Back Control

Setting Boundaries

Setting boundaries is a crucial step in taking back control of your life and breaking free from an abusive relationship. When you have been subjected to emotional abuse, manipulation, and control, it is essential to establish clear boundaries to protect yourself and maintain your well-being.

Understanding Boundaries

Boundaries are the limits we set for ourselves and others in terms of what is acceptable and what is not. They define our personal space, emotional needs, and values. In an abusive relationship, boundaries are often violated, disregarded, or manipulated by the abuser. This can leave the victim feeling powerless, confused, and without a sense of self.

Setting boundaries is about reclaiming your autonomy and asserting your rights as an individual. It involves recognizing and communicating your needs, desires, and limits to others. Establishing clear boundaries creates a framework for healthy relationships and protects yourself from further harm.

Identifying Your Boundaries

Before you can effectively set boundaries, it is important to identify what your boundaries are. Take some time to reflect on your values, needs, and what makes you feel comfortable or uncomfortable in a relationship. Consider the areas where you have felt violated or disrespected in the past. These can include emotional, physical, sexual, and financial boundaries.

Protecting your thoughts, feelings, and personal space is all part of having emotional boundaries. They include setting limits on how much emotional labor you are willing to invest in a relationship and what kind of behavior is acceptable or unacceptable.

Physical boundaries encompass your personal space and physical well-being. They involve setting limits on physical contact, personal belongings, and personal space invasion.

Sexual boundaries involve consent and the right to make decisions about your own body. They include setting limits on sexual activities and ensuring that all sexual encounters are consensual.

Financial boundaries involve having control over your finances and making decisions about how your money is spent. Among these are restrictions on the abuser's ability to manage and manipulate money.

Communicating Your Boundaries

Once you have identified your boundaries, it is important to communicate them clearly and assertively to your partner or others in your life. This can be a challenging task, especially if you have been conditioned to prioritize the needs and wants of others over your own.

When communicating your boundaries, being direct, specific, and firm is important. Use "I" statements to express your needs and feelings, such as "I feel uncomfortable when..." or "I need..." Avoid blaming or criticizing the other person, as this can lead to defensiveness and resistance.

It is also important to reinforce your boundaries with consistent actions. If your boundaries are repeatedly violated, it may be necessary to enforce consequences, such as distancing yourself from the person or ending the relationship altogether. Setting boundaries is about protecting yourself and creating a safe environment for your well-being.

Dealing with Resistance

The abuser may occasionally push back against or ignore your boundaries. They may try to manipulate or guilt-trip you into abandoning your boundaries. It is important to stay strong and assertive in these situations.

If the abuser continues to violate your boundaries, it may be necessary to seek support from a trusted friend, family member, or professional. They can provide guidance, and validation, and help you navigate the challenges of setting boundaries in an abusive relationship.

Rebuilding Self-Esteem and Confidence

Setting boundaries is about protecting yourself from further harm and rebuilding your self-esteem and confidence. When you assert your boundaries and see them respected, it reinforces your sense of self-worth and empowers you to take control of your life.

Setting boundaries is a process that takes time and practice. It is normal to feel uncomfortable or guilty at first, especially if you have been conditioned to prioritize the needs of others. Be patient with yourself and celebrate each small step you take towards reclaiming your autonomy and breaking free from the chains of abuse.

By setting and enforcing boundaries, you reclaim your power and pave the way for a healthier and more fulfilling future.

Assertiveness and Communication Skills

In an abusive relationship, one of the key factors that perpetuates the cycle of abuse is the lack of assertiveness and effective communication skills. Abusers often use manipulation, control, and intimidation tactics to silence their victims and maintain power and control over them. As a result, survivors of abuse may struggle to express their needs, set boundaries, and communicate effectively.

Assertiveness is the ability to express oneself confidently and directly while respecting the rights and boundaries of others. It involves standing up for oneself, expressing opinions, and asserting personal boundaries clearly and respectfully. Developing assertiveness skills is crucial for survivors of abuse as it empowers them to regain control over their lives and establish healthy relationships.

Understanding Assertiveness

Assertiveness is not about being aggressive or confrontational. It is about expressing oneself honestly and respectfully, without violating the rights of others. It involves being able to communicate one's needs, wants, and feelings clearly and directly, while also being open to listening to the perspectives of others.

Survivors of abuse often struggle with assertiveness due to the fear of retaliation or the belief that their opinions and needs are not valid. They may have been conditioned to believe that their voice doesn't matter or that expressing themselves will only lead to further harm. Learning to be assertive is an essential step toward breaking free from the chains of abuse.

Building Assertiveness Skills

Building assertiveness skills takes time and practice. Here are some strategies that can help survivors of abuse develop assertiveness and effective communication skills:

Self-awareness:

Developing self-awareness is the first step towards assertiveness. Take the time to reflect on your needs, values, and boundaries. Understand your rights as an individual and recognize that your opinions and feelings are valid.

Practice assertive communication:

Assertive communication involves expressing oneself clearly, directly, and respectfully. Use "I" statements to express your thoughts and feelings, such as "I feel..." or "I need...". Avoid blaming or attacking language and focus on expressing your needs assertively.

Set boundaries:

Setting boundaries is crucial in any relationship. Make it clear to yourself what conduct is appropriate and inappropriate. Communicate your boundaries assertively and be prepared to enforce them if they are violated.

Active listening:

Effective communication is a two-way process. You can engage in active listening by paying close attention to the speaker, keeping eye contact, and demonstrating empathy. Reflect on what the speaker has said to ensure understanding and validate their feelings.

Conflict resolution:

Conflict is a natural part of any relationship. Learning healthy conflict resolution skills can help survivors of abuse navigate difficult conversations assertively. Focus on finding mutually beneficial solutions and avoid resorting to aggression or passive-aggressive behavior.

Seek support:

Building assertiveness skills can be challenging, especially for survivors of abuse. Seek support from trusted friends, family members, or support groups who can encourage and guide your journey.

Overcoming Communication Barriers

Survivors of abuse often face unique communication barriers that can hinder their ability to express themselves assertively. These barriers may include:

Fear and anxiety:

The fear of retaliation or further abuse can make it difficult for survivors to speak up and assert themselves. It is important to address and manage these fears through therapy, support groups, or professional help.

Low self-esteem:

Abuse can severely impact a survivor's self-esteem, making them doubt their worth and abilities. Working on building self-esteem and self-confidence is crucial in overcoming communication barriers.

Emotional triggers:

Survivors may have emotional triggers that make it challenging to communicate effectively. These triggers can be reminders of past abuse or situations that evoke intense emotions. Learning coping mechanisms and self-regulation techniques can help manage these triggers.

Gaslighting and manipulation:

Abusers often employ gaslighting tactics to distort the survivor's perception of reality and undermine their confidence. Recognizing these manipulative tactics and seeking support can help survivors overcome the communication barriers created by gaslighting.

The Power of Assertiveness

Developing assertiveness and effective communication skills is a transformative process for survivors of abuse. It allows them to reclaim their voice, set boundaries, and establish healthy relationships based on mutual respect and equality.

By practicing assertiveness, survivors can break free from the chains of abuse and create a life filled with empowerment, self-worth, and healthy connections.

Assertiveness is a skill that can be learned and honed over time. It is a powerful tool that enables survivors to advocate for themselves, express their needs, and build a life free from abuse.

Developing Self-Esteem and Confidence

Developing self-esteem and confidence is a crucial step in breaking free from an abusive relationship. When you have been subjected to emotional abuse and manipulation, your self-worth and confidence may have been severely damaged. Rebuilding these aspects of yourself is essential for your healing and for creating a healthier future.

Understanding Self-Esteem

The way we view and regard ourselves is referred to as our self-esteem. It is the belief in our worth and abilities. The abuser frequently lowers your self-esteem in an abusive relationship, leading you to question your value and competence. It is important to recognize that the negative beliefs you may have about yourself are a result of the abuse and not a reflection of your true value as a person.

Challenging Negative Self-Talk

One of the first steps in developing self-esteem is to challenge and change the negative self-talk that has been ingrained in your mind. It's possible that the abuser continuously made fun of and criticized you, which caused you to internalize their bad sentiments. Start by becoming aware of the negative thoughts and beliefs you have about yourself. Then, consciously challenge them by replacing them with positive and affirming statements.

For example, if you catch yourself thinking, "I'm worthless," replace it with, "I am deserving of love and respect." Over time, this practice will help rewire your thinking patterns and build a more positive self-image.

Celebrating Your Strengths and Achievements

Abusive relationships often make you feel powerless and incapable. To counteract this, it is important to recognize and celebrate your strengths and achievements. Take some time to reflect on your accomplishments, no matter how small they may seem. This could be anything from completing a task at work to taking care of yourself during a difficult time.

By acknowledging your strengths and celebrating your achievements, you reinforce positive beliefs about yourself and build your self-esteem. You are capable of so much more than you may have been led to believe.

Practicing Self-Care

Self-care is an essential component of developing self-esteem and confidence. It involves taking care of your physical, emotional, and mental well-being. Engaging in activities that bring you joy and relaxation can help boost your self-esteem and remind you of your worth.

Make a list of activities that make you feel good and prioritize incorporating them into your daily routine. This could include things like exercising, spending time in nature, practicing mindfulness or meditation, journaling, or engaging in hobbies that bring you joy. Taking care of yourself sends a powerful message that you value and deserve to be treated with kindness and respect.

Surrounding Yourself with Positive Influences

The people we surround ourselves with can have a significant impact on our self-esteem and confidence. Surrounding yourself with positive influences can help uplift and support you on your journey of healing and self-discovery.

Seek out friends, family members, or support groups who are understanding, empathetic, and supportive. These individuals can provide a safe space for you to share your experiences and feelings without judgment. Their encouragement and validation can help you rebuild your self-esteem and remind you of your worth.

Setting Realistic Goals

Setting realistic goals is an important part of developing self-esteem and confidence. Start by identifying what you want to achieve in different areas of your life, such as career, relationships, and personal growth. Divide these objectives into more manageable chunks.

By setting and accomplishing realistic goals, you are proving to yourself that you are capable and deserving of success. Each small achievement will contribute to your overall sense of self-worth and confidence.

Seeking Professional Help

Sometimes, developing self-esteem and confidence may require professional guidance. Consider seeking therapy or counseling to work through the emotional wounds caused by the abusive relationship. A trained therapist can help you explore your feelings, challenge negative beliefs, and develop strategies to rebuild your self-esteem.

Therapy can provide a safe and supportive environment where you can process your experiences, gain insights, and learn new coping skills. Seeking help is not a sign of weakness but a courageous step towards healing and reclaiming your life.

Practicing Self-Compassion

Developing self-esteem and confidence also involves practicing self-compassion. As you move through the healing process, treat yourself with kindness and gentleness. Understand that healing takes time and that setbacks are a normal part of the journey.

When you make a mistake or face a challenge, treat yourself with the same compassion and understanding you would offer to a friend. Remind yourself that you are doing your best and deserve love, care, and forgiveness.

Embracing Your Authentic Self

In an abusive relationship, you may have lost touch with your authentic self. Take the time to reconnect with who you truly are and embrace your unique qualities and strengths. Engage in activities that align with your values and interests, and surround yourself with people who appreciate and support the real you.

By embracing your authentic self, you reclaim your power and build a strong foundation for self-esteem and confidence. You are worthy of love, respect, and happiness, and you have the strength within you to break free from the chains of abuse.

Managing Anger and Emotions

It can be quite difficult to control your anger and emotions in an abusive relationship. The cycle of abuse often involves the abuser using anger and emotional manipulation as a means of control. As a survivor, it is important to learn how to navigate and regulate your own emotions to break free from the cycle and regain control over your life.

Understanding Anger

Everyone experiences anger, which is a normal and natural emotion. However, rage is frequently employed as a tool to control and frighten the victim in abusive relationships. It is important to understand that anger is not inherently bad or wrong, but it is the way it is expressed that can be harmful.

Recognizing Triggers

One of the first steps in managing anger and emotions is to identify the triggers that lead to these intense feelings. Triggers can be specific situations, words, or actions that remind you of past abuse or cause you to feel threatened. By recognizing these triggers, you can begin to develop strategies to cope with them and prevent them from escalating into anger or emotional outbursts.

Developing Coping Mechanisms

Once you have identified your triggers, it is important to develop healthy coping mechanisms to manage your anger and emotions. These coping mechanisms can include deep breathing exercises, mindfulness techniques, journaling, or engaging in activities that bring you joy and relaxation. Finding healthy outlets for your emotions can help you release tension and prevent them from building up.

Seeking Professional Help

Managing anger and emotions can be a complex process, especially for survivors of abuse. It is important to seek professional help from therapists or counselors who specialize in trauma and domestic violence. They can provide the necessary tools and support to navigate your emotions and develop healthy coping strategies.

Expressing Emotions in a Healthy Way

Emotional expression in an abusive relationship may have unfavorable effects. As a survivor, learning how to express your emotions healthily and assertively is important. This involves setting boundaries and communicating your feelings calmly and respectfully. Learning effective communication skills can help you express your emotions without resorting to anger or aggression.

Practicing Self-Care

Taking care of yourself is crucial when it comes to managing anger and emotions. Engaging in self-care activities such as exercise, getting enough sleep, eating well, and practicing relaxation techniques can help reduce stress and promote emotional well-being. It is important to prioritize your own needs and make self-care a regular part of your routine.

Building a Support System

Having a strong support system is essential in managing anger and emotions. Surrounding yourself with trusted friends, family members, or support groups can provide you with a safe space to express your feelings and receive validation and understanding. They can also offer guidance and support as you navigate through the healing process.

Setting Boundaries

Setting boundaries is crucial in managing anger and emotions. It is important to establish clear boundaries with the abuser and communicate them assertively. This can help prevent situations that trigger anger and emotional distress. Setting boundaries also involves recognizing and respecting your limits and needs, and not allowing others to cross them.

Practicing Self-Reflection

Self-reflection is an important tool in managing anger and emotions. Taking the time to reflect on your thoughts, feelings, and reactions can help you gain insight into your triggers and patterns of behavior. It can also help you identify any negative thought patterns or beliefs that may be contributing to your anger. Self-reflection allows you to take responsibility for your own emotions and empowers you to make positive changes.

Seeking Emotional Support

Managing anger and emotions can be a challenging journey, and it is important to seek emotional support when needed. This can involve reaching out to a trusted friend, family member, or therapist who can provide a listening ear and offer guidance. Seeking emotional support can help you process your feelings and gain perspective on your experiences.

Managing anger and emotions takes time and practice. It is a journey of self-discovery and healing. By developing healthy coping mechanisms, seeking professional help, and building a strong support system, you can regain control over your emotions and break free from the chains of abuse.

Empowering Yourself

In an abusive relationship, the abuser often seeks to exert power and control over their partner. They may use various tactics such as manipulation, intimidation, and emotional abuse to maintain dominance. As a survivor, it is crucial to recognize that you have the power to break free from this cycle and regain control over your life. Empowering yourself is an essential step towards healing and creating a future free from abuse.

Understanding Your Worth

One of the first steps in empowering yourself is recognizing your worth. Abusers often try to diminish their partner's self-esteem and make them believe that they are unworthy or deserving of the abuse. It is important to understand that you are valuable and deserving of love, respect, and happiness.

Take the time to reflect on your strengths, talents, and achievements. Remind yourself of your worth and the positive qualities that make you unique. Surround yourself with supportive and loving people who can help reinforce your self-worth and remind you of your value.

Building Self-Confidence

Building self-confidence is another crucial aspect of empowering yourself. Abusers often try to undermine their partner's confidence, making them doubt their abilities and decisions. Rebuilding your self-confidence is a powerful way to regain control over your life.

Start by setting small, achievable goals for yourself. No matter how minor they may seem, acknowledge and celebrate your victories. Engage in activities that make you feel good about yourself, whether it's pursuing a hobby, learning a new skill, or taking care of your physical and mental well-being.

Surround yourself with positive influences and supportive individuals who believe in your abilities. Seek out empowering resources such as books, podcasts, or support groups that can help you develop a strong sense of self-confidence.

Educating Yourself

Knowledge is power, and educating yourself about abuse and its effects can be empowering. Understanding the dynamics of abuse, the tactics used by abusers, and the impact it has on survivors can help you make informed decisions and take necessary steps towards breaking free.

Read books, articles, and research about abusive relationships and the recovery process. Attend workshops or seminars that focus on empowering survivors and providing them with the tools to rebuild their lives. Educate yourself about your legal rights and the resources available to you, such as shelters, hotlines, and support services.

Setting Boundaries

Setting boundaries is an essential part of empowering yourself and reclaiming your autonomy. To stay in control, abusers frequently push their partners' limitations and ignore their boundaries. By establishing clear boundaries, you are asserting your right to be treated with respect and dignity.

Identify your boundaries and communicate them assertively to your partner. Be firm in enforcing these boundaries and do not compromise on your values or well-being. Surround yourself with people who respect your boundaries and support your journey towards empowerment.

Practicing Self-Care

Self-care is not selfish; it is a vital component of empowering yourself and healing from the trauma of abuse. Prioritizing your physical, emotional, and mental well-being is crucial in rebuilding your life and regaining control.

Take part in things that make you happy and relaxed. Practice self-compassion and be gentle with yourself as you navigate the healing process. Take care of your physical health by eating nutritious food, exercising regularly, and getting enough rest.

Seek professional help if needed, such as therapy or counseling, to address any emotional or psychological wounds caused by the abuse. Surround yourself with a support system that understands the importance of self-care and encourages you to prioritize your well-being.

Finding Your Voice

In an abusive relationship, the abuser often silences their partner's voice and opinions. Empowering yourself means finding your voice and reclaiming your right to express yourself freely.

Practice assertive communication skills to effectively express your thoughts, feelings, and needs. Speak up for yourself and advocate for your rights. Surround yourself with individuals who value your opinions and encourage you to use your voice.

Engage in activities that help you find your creative expression, such as writing, painting, or singing. Use your voice to share your story and raise awareness about abuse, helping others who may be going through similar experiences.

Embracing Independence

Empowering yourself also involves embracing your independence and reclaiming your autonomy. Abusers often try to isolate their partners and make them dependent on them for their basic needs. Breaking free from this cycle means rediscovering your independence and taking control of your life.

Take steps towards financial independence by seeking employment or pursuing education and training opportunities. Build a support network of friends, family, and professionals who can provide guidance and assistance as you navigate your journey toward independence.

Make decisions for yourself and trust your instincts. Embrace the freedom to choose your path and create a life that aligns with your values and aspirations. You have the power to shape your future and break free from the chains of abuse.

By empowering yourself, you are taking a courageous step towards reclaiming your life and creating a future filled with love, respect, and happiness.

Chapter 4: Leaving the Relationship

Understanding the Importance of Leaving

It takes bravery and difficulty to leave an abusive relationship. It is a step towards reclaiming your life, your happiness, and your freedom. Understanding the importance of leaving is crucial in breaking the chains of abuse and starting a new chapter filled with safety, peace, and self-love.

Breaking the Cycle of Abuse

One of the key reasons why leaving an abusive relationship is so important is to break the cycle of abuse. Abuse is a pattern of behavior that tends to repeat itself unless it is interrupted. By leaving the relationship, you are refusing to perpetuate the cycle and allowing yourself the opportunity to create a healthier and happier future.

Leaving an abusive relationship not only benefits you but also any children involved. Children who witness abuse are more likely to become victims or abusers themselves in the future. By leaving, you are protecting them from the harmful effects of witnessing violence and teaching them that abuse is not acceptable.

Prioritizing Your Safety and Well-being

Your first focus should always be your safety and well-being. Staying in an abusive relationship puts you at risk of physical, emotional, and psychological harm. To safeguard your safety and defend yourself against additional abuse, leaving is an essential first step.

Abusive relationships often escalate over time, and what may start as emotional abuse can quickly turn into physical violence. By leaving, you are removing yourself from a dangerous situation and allowing yourself to heal and rebuild your life.

Restoring Your Self-esteem and Confidence

Abuse can have a devastating impact on your self-esteem and confidence. Over time, the constant belittling, manipulation, and control can erode your sense of self-worth. Leaving the relationship is a powerful act of reclaiming your self-esteem and rebuilding your confidence.

By leaving, you are taking a stand against the abuse and affirming your worth as an individual. It is a step towards rediscovering your strengths, talents, and passions. It's possible to concentrate on your personal development and restore the confidence that was stolen from you when you leave an abusive relationship.

Regaining Control of Your Life

Abusive relationships are characterized by a significant power imbalance, with the abuser exerting control over every aspect of the victim's life. Leaving the relationship is a crucial step in regaining control over your own life.

By leaving, you are reclaiming your autonomy and freedom. You are no longer subjected to the constant manipulation, monitoring, and restrictions imposed by the abuser. Leaving allows you to make decisions for yourself, pursue your interests, and live life on your terms.

Creating a Healthy Future

Leaving an abusive relationship opens the door to a future filled with health, happiness, and fulfillment. It allows you to create a life free from fear, violence, and control.

By leaving, you are creating space for healthy relationships to enter your life. You can surround yourself with supportive and loving individuals who respect your boundaries and treat you with kindness.

Seeking Justice and Accountability

Ending an abusive relationship gives you the chance to hold the abuser responsible for their actions and pursue justice. It is important to remember that abuse is never your fault, and you have the right to seek legal protection and support.

By leaving, you can pursue legal avenues to ensure your safety and the safety of any children involved. This may include obtaining restraining orders, pressing charges, or seeking custody arrangements. You can demand justice for the harm you have suffered by leaving an abusive relationship.

Embracing a Life of Freedom and Happiness

Leaving an abusive relationship is a courageous step towards embracing a life of freedom and happiness. It is an opportunity to rediscover yourself, pursue your dreams, and create a future filled with joy and fulfillment.

By leaving, you are breaking free from the chains of abuse and opening yourself up to a world of possibilities. You deserve to live a life free from fear, violence, and control. Leaving an abusive relationship is the first step towards reclaiming your power and embracing the life you truly deserve.

Leaving an abusive relationship is not easy, and it may require careful planning and support. Reach out to trusted friends, family, or professionals who can provide guidance and assistance. You are not alone, and there is help available to support you on your journey to freedom and healing.

Planning Your Exit Strategy

Leaving an abusive relationship can be an incredibly challenging and dangerous process. It requires careful planning and consideration to ensure your safety and well-being. In this section, we will discuss the importance of planning your exit strategy and provide you with practical steps to help you navigate this difficult journey.

Assessing Your Situation

Before you begin planning your exit strategy, it is crucial to assess your situation and understand the level of danger you may be facing. Every abusive relationship is unique, and the risks involved can vary. Take the time to evaluate the severity of the abuse, the presence of any weapons, and the potential for escalation. If you believe your life is in immediate danger, it is essential to contact emergency services or a local domestic violence hotline for immediate assistance.

Gathering Important Documents

When preparing to leave an abusive relationship, it is vital to gather all necessary documents and keep them in a safe place. These documents may include identification papers (such as your passport, driver's license, and social security card), financial records, bank statements, insurance policies, and any evidence of abuse (such as photographs, emails, or text messages). Having these documents readily available will make it easier for you to establish your independence and protect your rights.

Securing Your Finances

Financial independence is crucial when leaving an abusive relationship. Abusers often use financial control as a means of maintaining power and control over their victims. Take steps to secure your finances by opening a separate bank account in your name only, ensuring that your paycheck or any other income goes directly into this account. If possible, set aside some money for emergencies or seek assistance from local organizations that provide financial support to survivors of abuse.

Establishing a Support Network

Leaving an abusive relationship can be an overwhelming and isolating experience. Building a strong support network is essential during this time. Reach out to trusted friends, family members, or support groups who can provide emotional support, practical assistance, and a safe place to stay if needed. Let them know about your situation and your plans to leave, so they can be prepared to help you when the time comes.

Creating a Safety Plan

A safety plan is a personalized strategy that outlines the steps you will take to protect yourself and your children, if applicable, during and after leaving the abusive relationship. It is essential to create a safety plan that is tailored to your specific circumstances. Some key elements to consider when developing your safety plan include:

Identifying safe places to go in case of an emergency, such as a trusted friend's house, a shelter, or a public space.

Memorizing important phone numbers, including those of local law enforcement, domestic violence hotlines, and your support network.

Putting your belongings in a secure location where your abuser cannot locate them, and filling a backpack with necessities including clothing, toiletries, critical documents, and any required prescriptions.

Planning your escape route and practicing it to ensure you can leave quickly and safely if necessary.

Changing your routines and varying your daily activities make it more difficult for your abuser to track your movements.

Seeking Legal Protection

Obtaining legal protection is an important step in ensuring your safety and holding your abuser accountable for their actions. Consult with a lawyer or a local domestic violence organization to understand your legal rights and options.

They can assist you in obtaining an order of protection or restraining order, which can limit your abuser's access to you and offer legal protection. Keep a copy of these legal documents with you at all times and share them with trusted individuals who may need to be aware of the situation.

Documenting the Abuse

Documenting the abuse you have experienced can be crucial when seeking legal protection or support. Maintain a thorough log of all occurrences, including the dates, times, places, and specifics of the abuse. If possible, take photographs of any visible injuries or property damage. Save any written evidence, such as threatening messages or emails. These records can serve as valuable evidence should you decide to pursue legal action or seek assistance from law enforcement.

Leaving Safely

The riskiest period for survivors is when they leave an abusive relationship. It is essential to prioritize your safety above all else. If possible, plan your departure when your abuser is not present or when they are least likely to suspect your intentions. Consider enlisting the help of local law enforcement or a domestic violence hotline to ensure a safe exit. If you have children, develop a plan for their safety as well, including how you will communicate with them and ensure their well-being during the transition.

Regaining control over your life and breaking free from the bonds of abuse requires bravery, which is demonstrated by leaving an abusive relationship. It is important to have patience and compassion for yourself throughout this process. Seek support from professionals, friends, and family members who can provide guidance and encouragement.

Legal Protection and Resources

When you are in an abusive relationship, it is crucial to understand that you have legal rights and access to resources that can help protect you and support you in leaving the relationship.

Understanding Legal Protection

One of the first steps in leaving an abusive relationship is to understand the legal protections that are available to you. Laws vary from country to country and even from state to state, so it is important to familiarize yourself with the specific laws in your jurisdiction. Here are some common legal protections that may be available to you:

Restraining Orders or Protection Orders

A restraining order, also known as a protection order, is a legal document that prohibits the abuser from contacting or coming near you. It can provide you with a sense of safety and security by legally mandating that the abuser stay away from you, your home, your workplace, and your children. Restraining orders can also include provisions for child custody and visitation, as well as financial support.

To obtain a restraining order, you will typically need to go to your local courthouse and file a petition. The process may involve providing evidence of the abuse, such as police reports, medical records, or witness statements. It is important to consult with an attorney or a domestic violence advocate who can guide you through the process and help you gather the necessary documentation.

Divorce and Child Custody

If you are married to your abuser and have children together, you may need to consider filing for divorce and seeking custody of your children. Divorce can be a complex legal process, especially when domestic violence is involved. It is important to consult with an attorney who specializes in family law and domestic violence to ensure that your rights and the best interests of your children are protected.

Courts take domestic violence allegations seriously when determining child custody arrangements. They prioritize the safety and well-being of the children and may consider factors such as the history of abuse, the abuser's ability to provide a safe and stable environment, and the children's preferences (if they are old enough to express them). An attorney can help you navigate the legal process and advocate for your rights as a parent.

Criminal Charges

If your abuser is committing serious acts of violence or abuse, you may decide to file criminal charges. This can lead to their arrest, prosecution, and potentially a conviction. It is important to report incidents of abuse to the police as soon as possible and provide them with any evidence you have, such as photographs, medical records, or witness statements. Working with law enforcement and prosecutors can help ensure that your abuser is held accountable for their actions.

Resources for Survivors

The process of ending an abusive relationship can be difficult and exhausting. Fortunately, there are numerous resources available to survivors of abuse that can provide support, guidance, and assistance. Here are some key resources to consider:

Domestic Violence Hotlines

Domestic violence hotlines offer victims of abuse discreet help and information around the clock. Trained advocates can help you develop a safety plan, provide emotional support, and connect you with local resources such as shelters, counseling services, and legal aid. Hotlines can be a lifeline for those in crisis and can offer immediate support when needed.

Shelters and Safe Houses

Shelters and safe houses provide temporary housing and support services for individuals fleeing abusive relationships. They offer a safe and confidential environment where survivors and their children can stay while they plan their next steps. Shelters often provide a range of services, including counseling, legal advocacy, support groups, and assistance with finding permanent housing. Contact your local domestic violence hotline or search online for shelters in your area.

Counseling and Therapy

Seeking counseling or therapy can be instrumental in the healing and recovery process after leaving an abusive relationship. Therapists who specialize in trauma and domestic violence can help you process your experiences, rebuild your self-esteem, and develop healthy coping mechanisms. They can also provide support as you navigate the legal process and make important decisions about your future.

Legal Aid Organizations

Those who cannot afford private attorneys can receive free or inexpensive legal services from legal aid organizations. They can provide legal advice, help with filing restraining orders or divorce papers, and represent you in court if necessary. Contact your local legal aid organization to inquire about their services and eligibility requirements.

Support Groups

Joining a support group can be incredibly beneficial as you navigate the challenges of leaving an abusive relationship. Support groups provide a safe and non-judgmental space where survivors can share their experiences, gain support from others who have been through similar situations, and learn coping strategies. Many domestic violence organizations offer support groups, both in-person and online.

Understanding your legal rights and accessing available resources is crucial when leaving an abusive relationship. Restraining orders, divorce proceedings, and criminal charges can provide legal protection, while domestic violence hotlines, shelters, counseling services, legal aid organizations, and support groups can offer the support and assistance you need. You are not alone, and there are people and organizations ready to help you break free from the chains of abuse.

Leaving Safely

Leaving an abusive relationship can be a challenging and dangerous process. It is crucial to prioritize your safety and take necessary precautions to ensure a smooth transition out of the relationship.

Assessing the Risk

Before making any plans to leave, it is essential to assess the level of risk involved. Every abusive relationship is unique, and the danger can vary depending on the abuser's behavior and history. When assessing the risk, take into account the following factors:

History of Violence: If your partner has a history of physical violence or has threatened to harm you in the past, the risk of danger is higher.

Control and Possessiveness: If your partner exhibits controlling and possessive behaviors, such as monitoring your activities, isolating you from friends and family, or restricting your access to resources, leaving may escalate their abusive behavior.

Escalating Abuse: If the abuse has been escalating over time, it is crucial to take extra precautions when leaving, as the abuser may become more desperate to maintain control.

Threats and Intimidation: If your partner has made threats to harm you, your children, or your loved ones, it is essential to take these threats seriously and plan accordingly.

Access to Weapons: If your partner has access to firearms or other weapons, the risk of severe harm or fatality increases significantly.

By assessing these factors, you can gain a better understanding of the potential risks involved and make informed decisions about your safety.

Creating a Safety Plan

A safety plan is a crucial tool that can help you navigate the process of leaving an abusive relationship. It involves developing a strategy to protect yourself and minimize the risk of harm. Here are some steps to consider when creating a safety plan:

Identify Safe Spaces: Determine safe places where you can go in case of an emergency. This could include the homes of trusted friends or family members, domestic violence shelters, or hotels.

Pack an Emergency Bag: Prepare a bag with essential items that you may need when leaving quickly. This could include identification documents, money, a change of clothes, important phone numbers, medications, and any necessary legal documents.

Secure Your Communication: Change your passwords for email, social media, and other online accounts. Consider using a secure communication app or creating a new email address that your abuser does not know about.

Inform Trusted Individuals: Reach out to trusted friends, family members, or neighbors and inform them about your situation. Share your safety plan with them and provide them with copies of any relevant documents.

Document Evidence: Any instances of abuse should be documented, along with the dates, times, and details. Take pictures of any damage to property or injuries. This documentation can be crucial if you decide to involve law enforcement or seek legal protection.

Restraining Orders and Legal Protection: Research the process of obtaining a restraining order or other legal protections available in your jurisdiction. Consult with a lawyer or a local domestic violence organization for guidance on how to proceed.

Change Your Routine: Change your daily schedule to avoid spending as much time with your abuser. This could include changing your work schedule, taking different routes, or avoiding places where you are likely to encounter them.

Practice Self-Care: Prioritize self-care during this challenging time. Engage in activities that bring you joy and help reduce stress. Seek support from therapists, support groups, or helplines specializing in domestic violence.

A safety plan should be tailored to your specific circumstances. It is essential to regularly reassess and update your plan as needed.

Seeking Support

Leaving an abusive relationship can be an overwhelming and emotionally draining experience. It is crucial to seek support from trusted individuals and organizations who can provide guidance and assistance. Here are some sources of support to consider:

Friends and Family: Reach out to trusted friends and family members who can offer emotional support, provide a safe place to stay, or help you with practical matters.

Domestic Violence Hotlines: Get in touch with regional or national hotlines that specialize in domestic abuse. They can provide you with information, resources, and emotional support 24/7.

Therapists and Counselors: Seek professional help from therapists or counselors who specialize in trauma and domestic violence. They can help you process your emotions, develop coping strategies, and rebuild your life.

Support Groups: Join support groups for survivors of domestic violence. Connecting with others who have experienced similar situations can provide validation, understanding, and a sense of community.

Domestic Violence Organizations: Reach out to local domestic violence organizations that offer a range of services, including emergency shelter, legal advocacy, counseling, and support groups.

This is not a process you have to go through alone. Seeking support is a sign of strength and can greatly assist you in navigating the challenges of leaving an abusive relationship.

Leaving with Children

If you have children, leaving an abusive relationship requires additional considerations to ensure their safety. Here are some important steps to take when leaving with children:

Safety Planning: Develop a safety plan specifically tailored to your children's needs. Consider their age, school routines, and any special requirements they may have.

Legal Considerations: Consult with a lawyer or a local domestic violence organization to understand your rights and legal options regarding custody, visitation, and child support.

School and Childcare: Inform your children's school or childcare providers about the situation and provide them with copies of any relevant legal documents, such as restraining orders or custody agreements.

Emergency Contacts: Ensure that your children have access to emergency contact information, including trusted adults they can reach out to if they feel unsafe or threatened.

Therapeutic Support: Seek therapeutic support for your children to help them process their emotions and experiences. Child therapists who specialize in trauma can provide valuable guidance and assistance.

Rebuilding Stability: Focus on creating a stable and nurturing environment for your children. Establish routines, provide emotional support, and engage in activities that promote their well-being.

Leaving an abusive relationship with children can be complex, but prioritizing their safety and well-being is crucial. Reach out to professionals and organizations specializing in domestic violence to ensure you have the necessary support and resources.

It takes bravery to leave an abusive relationship to take back your life and escape the abuse's hold. Your safety and well-being are paramount, and there are people and resources available to support you throughout this journey.

Chapter 5: Healing and Recovery

Processing Trauma and Grief

The road to recovery from an abusive relationship is difficult and multifaceted. It is not only about leaving the toxic environment but also about healing the deep emotional wounds caused by the trauma. Processing trauma and grief is a crucial step towards reclaiming your life and finding inner peace.

Understanding Trauma

Trauma is an extremely upsetting or stressful event that surpasses your capacity for adjustment. In an abusive relationship, trauma can manifest in various forms, including physical, emotional, and psychological abuse. It is important to recognize that trauma affects individuals differently, and there is no right or wrong way to experience it. Some common reactions to trauma include:

- Flashbacks and intrusive memories
- Nightmares and sleep disturbances

- Hypervigilance and constant fear

- Avoidance of triggers or reminders

- Emotional numbness or detachment

- Difficulty trusting others

Seeking Professional Help

Processing trauma and grief often requires professional support. Therapists and counselors who specialize in trauma can provide a safe and non-judgmental space for you to explore your emotions and experiences. They can help you develop coping mechanisms, process your feelings, and work towards healing and recovery. Some common therapeutic approaches for trauma include:

- Cognitive Behavioral Therapy (CBT): This therapy focuses on identifying and changing negative thought patterns and behaviors that contribute to distress.

- Eye Movement Desensitization and Reprocessing (EMDR): EMDR helps process traumatic memories by using bilateral stimulation to stimulate the brain's natural healing mechanisms.

- Trauma-Focused Cognitive Behavioral Therapy (TF-CBT): This therapy combines cognitive-behavioral techniques with trauma-focused interventions to address the impact of trauma on thoughts, emotions, and behaviors.

Expressive Therapies

Expressive therapies can be powerful tools for processing trauma and grief. These therapies utilize creative outlets to help individuals explore and express their emotions in a non-verbal way. Some common expressive therapies include:

Art therapy: Using various art forms such as painting, drawing, or sculpting to express emotions and explore inner experiences.

Music therapy: Engaging in music-related activities, such as listening, playing instruments, or songwriting, to promote emotional expression and healing.

Dance/movement therapy: Using movement and dance to connect with emotions, release tension, and promote self-expression.

Self-Care and Self-Compassion

Taking care of yourself is essential during the healing process. Self-care involves prioritizing your physical, emotional, and mental well-being. Here are some self-care practices that can support your healing journey:

Establishing a routine: Creating a structured daily routine can provide a sense of stability and control.

Engaging in relaxation techniques: Practicing deep breathing exercises, meditation, or mindfulness can help reduce anxiety and promote relaxation.

Nurturing your body: Engage in activities that promote physical well-being, such as regular exercise, healthy eating, and getting enough sleep.

Engaging in activities you enjoy: Pursue hobbies and activities that bring you joy and help you reconnect with your interests and passions.

Setting boundaries: Learn to say no and prioritize your needs. Establishing healthy boundaries is crucial for self-care and protecting your emotional well-being.

Building a Support Network

Having a strong support network is vital for healing from trauma and grief. Surrounding yourself with understanding and empathetic individuals can provide validation, encouragement, and a sense of belonging. Here are a few strategies for creating a network of support:

Reach out to friends and family: Share your experiences with trusted loved ones who can provide emotional support and understanding.

Join support groups: Connect with others who have experienced similar trauma through support groups or online communities. Sharing your stories and listening to others can be incredibly healing.

Seek professional support: Therapists and counselors can offer guidance, validation, and tools for healing. They can also help you connect with local support groups or resources.

Practicing Mindfulness and Grounding Techniques

Mindfulness and grounding techniques can help you stay present and manage overwhelming emotions. These practices can provide a sense of stability and help you regain control during moments of distress. The following are some methods you can try:

Deep breathing exercises: Focus on your breath, taking slow, deep breaths in and out. This can assist in bringing you back to the present moment and calming your nervous system.

Grounding exercises: Engage your senses by focusing on the physical sensations around you. Take note of the fragrances in the air, the noises in your surroundings, and the textures of objects.

Mindful meditation: Set aside time each day to practice mindfulness meditation. This entails focusing your attention on the here and now while avoiding passing judgment.

Healing from trauma and grief takes time. Be patient and compassionate with yourself as you navigate through the ups and downs of the healing process. With the right support, self-care practices, and professional guidance, you can gradually process your trauma, find inner strength, and move towards a healthier and happier future.

Rebuilding Trust in Relationships

Every happy and productive relationship starts with trust. However, after being in an abusive relationship, trust can be destroyed and is hard to regain. The scars left by emotional, physical, or psychological abuse can make it challenging to trust others again. But with time, patience, and self-care, it is possible to rebuild trust and create healthy relationships in your life.

Understanding the Impact of Abuse on Trust

Abuse can have a profound impact on your ability to trust others. When you have been betrayed, manipulated, or hurt by someone you loved and trusted, it is natural to become guarded and skeptical in future relationships. The fear of being hurt again can make it difficult to open up and trust others.

It is important to recognize that rebuilding trust takes time and healing. It is not something that can be completed quickly. It requires self-reflection, self-compassion, and a willingness to take small steps toward trusting others again.

Healing from Past Trauma

Before you can rebuild trust in relationships, it is crucial to heal from the trauma of the abusive relationship. This involves processing the emotions and pain associated with the abuse and finding healthy ways to cope with them.

Therapy can be a valuable tool in this healing process. A trained therapist can help you navigate through complex emotions and provide guidance on how to heal from the trauma. They can also help you develop healthy coping mechanisms and strategies to rebuild trust.

Taking care of oneself can help the healing process. This can include practicing mindfulness, engaging in hobbies that bring you joy, and surrounding yourself with supportive and understanding people.

Learning to Trust Yourself

Rebuilding trust in relationships starts with learning to trust yourself again. When you have been in an abusive relationship, your self-esteem and self-worth may have been severely damaged. It is important to work on rebuilding your self-confidence and belief in your judgment.

One way to do this is by setting boundaries and honoring them. By setting clear boundaries and enforcing them, you are sending a message to yourself and others that your needs and well-being are important. This can help you regain a sense of control and trust in your decision-making.

It is also important to practice self-compassion and forgiveness. Recognize that the abuse was not your fault and that you deserve love, respect, and healthy relationships. Be patient with yourself as you navigate the healing process and remember that it is okay to make mistakes along the way.

Taking Small Steps Towards Trust

Rebuilding trust in relationships is a gradual process that requires taking small steps. It is important to start with low-risk situations and gradually work your way up to more vulnerable ones.

Begin by surrounding yourself with supportive and trustworthy individuals. This can include friends, family members, or support groups who understand and validate your experiences. Building a strong support system can provide a safe space for you to practice trusting others again.

As you feel more comfortable, you can start opening up and sharing your thoughts and feelings with others. Start with small disclosures and observe how the other person responds. Pay attention to their actions and words, and gradually build trust based on their consistency and reliability.

Communicating and Building Transparency

Open and honest communication is essential in rebuilding trust in relationships. It is important to express your needs, concerns, and boundaries clearly to the other person. This allows for open dialogue and helps establish a foundation of trust.

Building transparency is also crucial. This means being open about your past experiences and any triggers or vulnerabilities that may arise as a result. By sharing this information with your partner or loved ones, they can better understand your needs and provide the support you require.

Patience and Understanding

Rebuilding trust takes time, and it is important to be patient with yourself and others. Understand that trust is earned and that it may take longer for you to fully trust again. It is okay to have moments of doubt or fear, but it is important to communicate these feelings with your partner or loved ones.

It is also important to remember that not everyone will be deserving of your trust. Trust should be earned through consistent actions and behaviors over time. If someone repeatedly violates your boundaries or fails to show respect and understanding, it may be necessary to reevaluate the relationship.

Seeking Professional Help

If you find that rebuilding trust is particularly challenging or if you are struggling with unresolved trauma, seeking professional help can be beneficial. A therapist or counselor can provide guidance, support, and tools to help you navigate the process of rebuilding trust.

Therapy can also help you address any underlying issues that may be hindering your ability to trust, such as low self-esteem or unresolved trauma. A trained professional can assist you in developing healthy coping mechanisms and strategies to rebuild trust in relationships.

Rebuilding trust is a personal journey, and everyone's timeline will be different. Be kind to yourself, celebrate your progress, and surround yourself with people who support and uplift you. With time and self-care, you can rebuild trust and create healthy, fulfilling relationships in your life.

Self-Care and Self-Compassion

Self-care and self-compassion are essential aspects of healing and recovery from an abusive relationship. When you have experienced emotional abuse, manipulation, and control, it is crucial to prioritize your well-being and nurture yourself.

Prioritizing Your Needs

In an abusive relationship, your needs may have been consistently disregarded or invalidated. It is time to shift your focus back to yourself and prioritize your well-being. Self-care involves recognizing and meeting your physical, emotional, and mental needs. Start by identifying what brings you joy, peace, and fulfillment. This could be engaging in activities you love, spending time with supportive friends and family, or practicing mindfulness and relaxation techniques.

Self-care is essential to your recovery process; it is not selfish. By taking care of yourself, you are better equipped to handle the challenges that may arise as you move forward. Make a conscious effort to incorporate self-care activities into your daily routine, even if it is just for a few minutes each day. It could be as simple as taking a warm bath, going for a walk in nature, or journaling your thoughts and feelings.

Practicing Self-Compassion

The practice of showing yourself love, tolerance, and acceptance is known as self-compassion. It involves acknowledging your pain and suffering without judgment and offering yourself the same compassion you would extend to a dear friend. When you have been in an abusive relationship, it is common to blame yourself or feel ashamed. It is important to remember that you are not to blame for the abuse you endured.

Practice self-compassion by challenging negative self-talk and replacing it with self-affirming statements. Remind yourself that you are worthy of love, respect, and happiness. Be patient with yourself as you navigate the healing process, and allow yourself to feel and process your emotions without judgment. Surround yourself with supportive and understanding individuals who can provide a safe space for you to express yourself.

Setting Healthy Boundaries

Setting healthy boundaries is an essential aspect of self-care and self-compassion. It entails letting people know your requirements, boundaries, and expectations while also respecting theirs. In an abusive relationship, boundaries are often violated, and your autonomy is undermined. By establishing and enforcing healthy boundaries, you regain control over your life and protect yourself from further harm.

Start by identifying your boundaries and what feels comfortable and safe for you. Communicate these boundaries assertively and firmly to others, including friends, family, and potential romantic partners. It is important to remember that setting boundaries is not about being selfish or controlling; it is about taking care of yourself and ensuring your well-being.

Nurturing Your Physical Health

Taking care of your physical health is an integral part of self-care and self-compassion. Abuse can take a toll on your physical well-being, so it is crucial to prioritize your health as you heal and recover. Make sure you are receiving adequate rest, eating a balanced diet, and exercising regularly. Physical exercise not only improves your physical health but also releases endorphins, which can boost your mood and overall well-being.

Consider seeking medical attention to address any physical injuries or health concerns that may have resulted from the abuse. Regular check-ups and consultations with healthcare professionals can help you regain control over your physical health and provide you with the necessary support and guidance.

Cultivating Emotional Well-being

Emotional well-being is a vital aspect of self-care and self-compassion. After experiencing emotional abuse, it is common to feel a range of emotions, including sadness, anger, fear, and confusion. It's okay to feel and process these feelings without passing judgment on yourself. Seek support from trusted friends, family, or a therapist who can provide a safe space for you to express yourself and work through your emotions.

Engaging in activities that promote emotional well-being can also be beneficial. This could include practicing mindfulness and meditation, journaling, engaging in creative outlets such as art or music, or participating in support groups with individuals who have had similar experiences.

Practicing Self-Reflection and Growth

Self-care and self-compassion involve continuous self-reflection and personal growth. Take time to reflect on your experiences, identify patterns, and understand how the abusive relationship has impacted you. This self-reflection can help you gain insight into your strengths, weaknesses, and areas for growth.

As you embark on your healing journey, consider setting personal goals and aspirations for yourself. These goals can be small or significant, depending on your circumstances. Recognize your progress and celebrate the victories you have made along the path. Recovering is a non-linear process, and obstacles could arise. Be gentle with yourself and continue to practice self-compassion as you navigate the ups and downs of your recovery.

Building a Support Network

Building a strong support network is crucial for your healing and recovery. Surround yourself with individuals who uplift and support you, and who understand the challenges you have faced. Seek out support groups, counseling services, or online communities where you can connect with others who have had similar experiences. Sharing your story and listening to the experiences of others can provide validation, encouragement, and a sense of belonging.

You are not alone, and some people genuinely care about your well-being. Reach out to trusted friends, family, or professionals when you need support or guidance. Building a support network can help you feel empowered, validated, and understood as you continue on your journey of healing and recovery.

Self-care and self-compassion are essential components of healing and recovery from an abusive relationship. Prioritizing your needs, practicing self-compassion, setting healthy boundaries, nurturing your physical health, cultivating emotional well-being, practicing self-reflection and growth, and building a support network are all crucial steps in your path to recovery and life restoration.

Be patient with yourself, celebrate your progress, and seek professional help when needed. You deserve to live a life free from abuse and filled with love, respect, and happiness.

Seeking Therapy and Support Groups

Seeking therapy and joining support groups can be crucial steps in the healing and recovery process after leaving an abusive relationship. These resources provide a safe and supportive environment where survivors can share their experiences, gain valuable insights, and receive professional guidance to rebuild their lives.

The Benefits of Therapy

Therapy offers survivors of abusive relationships a space to process their trauma, explore their emotions, and develop coping strategies. A trained therapist can help survivors navigate the complex emotions that arise after leaving an abusive relationship, such as fear, anger, guilt, and sadness. They can also assist in identifying and addressing any underlying issues that may have contributed to the abusive relationship.

One of the primary benefits of therapy is the opportunity to gain a deeper understanding of oneself and the dynamics of abusive relationships. Through therapy, survivors can learn to recognize patterns of abuse, understand the impact it has had on their self-esteem and self-worth, and develop healthier relationship skills.

Therapy can also provide survivors with tools to manage anxiety, depression, and post-traumatic stress disorder (PTSD) symptoms that often accompany the aftermath of an abusive relationship. By working with a therapist, survivors can develop effective coping mechanisms and regain a sense of control over their lives.

Types of Therapy

Various types of therapy can be beneficial for survivors of abusive relationships. Some common approaches include:

Cognitive-behavioral therapy (CBT)

The goal of CBT is to recognize and alter harmful thinking patterns and behavior patterns. It helps survivors challenge distorted beliefs about themselves and their relationships, develop healthier coping strategies, and build resilience.

Trauma-Focused Therapy

Trauma-focused therapy is specifically designed to address the psychological impact of trauma. It helps survivors process their traumatic experiences, reduce distressing symptoms, and develop skills to manage triggers and flashbacks.

Dialectical Behavior Therapy (DBT)

DBT combines elements of cognitive-behavioral therapy with mindfulness techniques. It helps survivors regulate their emotions, improve interpersonal skills, and develop self-compassion.

Group Therapy

Group therapy provides survivors with a supportive community of individuals who have experienced similar challenges. It offers a safe space to share experiences, gain validation, and learn from others. Group therapy can be particularly beneficial in reducing feelings of isolation and building a sense of belonging.

Finding a Therapist

Finding the right therapist is essential for survivors seeking therapy. Here are some steps to consider:

Research: Look for therapists who specialize in trauma, abuse, or relationship issues. Online directories, professional organizations, and recommendations from trusted sources can help find qualified therapists.

Initial Consultation: Schedule an initial consultation with potential therapists to discuss your needs, goals, and concerns. This meeting will help you determine if the therapist is a good fit for you.

Trust and Connection: It is crucial to feel comfortable and safe with your therapist. Trust your instincts and choose someone with whom you can establish a strong therapeutic alliance.

Credentials and Experience: Ensure that the therapist is licensed and has experience working with survivors of abuse. Ask about their therapeutic approach and any specialized training they have received.

Cost and Accessibility: Consider the cost of therapy and whether the therapist accepts insurance or offers sliding scale fees. Additionally, assess the therapist's location and availability to ensure it aligns with your needs.

Support Groups

Support groups provide survivors with a sense of community and understanding. They offer a space to share experiences, receive validation, and learn from others who have gone through similar situations. Support groups can be in-person or online, and they can be facilitated by professionals or run by survivors themselves.

For survivors, joining a support group can be very helpful because it:

- Reduces feelings of isolation and loneliness
- Offers a secure environment for sharing experiences and expressing feelings
- Offers support and encouragement from others who have faced similar challenges
- Provides practical advice and coping strategies from individuals who have successfully rebuilt their lives

- Helps survivors develop a sense of empowerment and resilience

When considering a support group, it is important to find one that aligns with your specific needs and preferences. Some groups may focus on general support, while others may cater to specific demographics or types of abuse. Research local resources, reach out to community organizations, or ask your therapist for recommendations.

The Importance of Self-Care

While therapy and support groups are essential components of the healing process, it is equally important to prioritize self-care. Practicing self-care entails doing things that enhance one's mental, emotional, and physical health. It can include practices such as exercise, meditation, journaling, spending time in nature, and engaging in hobbies or creative outlets.

Self-care is crucial for survivors as it helps restore a sense of balance and nurtures their overall well-being. It is a way to honor oneself and prioritize personal needs and desires. By practicing self-care, survivors can rebuild their self-esteem, regain a sense of identity, and cultivate a positive relationship with themselves.

Seeking therapy and joining support groups are powerful steps towards healing and recovery, but they are just one part of the journey. Each survivor's path is unique, and it is important to be patient and compassionate with oneself throughout the process. With time, support, and self-care, survivors can break free from the chains of abuse and create a life filled with healing, growth, and empowerment.

Chapter 6: Moving Forward

Setting Goals and Creating a New Life

One of the most important steps in recovering and moving on from an abusive relationship is setting goals and starting a new life. It allows survivors to regain control over their lives, rebuild their self-esteem, and create a future that is free from abuse.

The Importance of Setting Goals

Setting goals is crucial for survivors of abusive relationships as it provides a sense of direction and purpose. It allows individuals to focus their energy on positive outcomes and helps them regain a sense of control over their lives. By setting goals, survivors can break free from the cycle of abuse and create a new life that is filled with happiness, fulfillment, and personal growth.

Setting Realistic and Achievable Goals

When setting goals, it is important to be realistic and consider the current circumstances and resources available. Survivors may have experienced significant emotional, financial, and psychological damage as a result of the abuse, so it is crucial to set goals that are attainable within their current situation. Here are some steps to help survivors set realistic and achievable goals:

Reflect on Personal Values and Priorities

Think carefully about your priorities and personal values. What is truly important to you? What are your passions and interests? Understanding your values and priorities will help you set goals that align with your authentic self.

Start Small and Build Momentum

Begin by setting small, easily achievable goals. This will help build confidence and momentum as you progress towards larger goals. Celebrate each accomplishment, no matter how small, as it will reinforce your belief in your ability to create positive change.

Break Goals into Manageable Steps

Break down larger goals into smaller, manageable steps. This will help to make the procedure more manageable and less intimidating. Each step achieved will bring you closer to your ultimate goal, providing a sense of progress and accomplishment.

Seek Support and Guidance

Reach out to a trusted friend, family member, or therapist who can provide support and guidance as you set and work towards your goals. Having someone to lean on during this process can be invaluable and provide the encouragement needed to stay motivated.

Steps to Creating a New Life

Creating a new life after leaving an abusive relationship involves taking intentional steps toward personal growth, healing, and rebuilding. Here are some steps to help survivors create a new life:

Focus on Self-Care

Prioritize self-care and make it a daily practice. This includes taking care of your physical, emotional, and mental well-being. Engage in activities that bring you joy, practice mindfulness and relaxation techniques, and ensure you are meeting your basic needs.

Explore New Interests and Hobbies

Take the opportunity to explore new interests and hobbies. This can be a chance to discover new passions and talents, as well as meet new people who share similar interests. Engaging in activities that bring you happiness and fulfillment will contribute to your overall well-being.

Build a Supportive Network

Surround yourself with a supportive network of friends, family, and professionals who understand and validate your experiences. Building healthy relationships and connections will provide you with the support and encouragement needed to navigate the challenges of creating a new life.

Set Career and Educational Goals

Consider setting career and educational goals that align with your interests and aspirations. This may involve furthering your education, seeking new job opportunities, or starting your own business. Investing in your professional growth can provide financial stability and a sense of purpose.

Practice Self-Reflection and Growth

Engage in self-reflection and personal growth activities. This may include journaling, therapy, or participating in support groups. By exploring your emotions, thoughts, and behaviors, you can gain a deeper understanding of yourself and continue to heal and grow.

Embrace Change and Take Risks

Embrace change and be open to taking calculated risks. Leaving an abusive relationship is a significant step towards creating a new life, and it requires courage and resilience. Embracing change and stepping outside of your comfort zone can lead to new opportunities and personal growth.

Celebrate Progress and Achievements

Celebrate your progress and achievements along the way. Recognize and acknowledge the steps you have taken to create a new life for yourself. Celebrating your accomplishments will reinforce your belief in your ability to overcome challenges and create a future filled with happiness and fulfillment.

By setting goals and creating a new life, survivors of abusive relationships can break free from the chains of their past and embrace a future filled with hope, empowerment, and personal growth.

Building Healthy Relationships

Building wholesome relationships is a vital part of moving on from an abusive relationship. It is a process that requires self-reflection, growth, and a commitment to creating a positive and supportive environment.

Self-Reflection and Healing

Before entering into a new relationship, it is crucial to take the time to heal and reflect on the past. Healing from an abusive relationship involves processing the trauma, rebuilding self-esteem, and learning to trust again. It is essential to address any unresolved emotions and seek therapy or support groups to aid in the healing process.

Self-reflection is also vital in understanding your own needs, values, and boundaries. Take the time to identify what you want and need in a healthy relationship. Reflect on the patterns and dynamics that were present in the abusive relationship and make a conscious effort to break those patterns.

Communication and Active Listening

A strong relationship is built on effective communication. It involves expressing your thoughts, feelings, and needs openly and honestly while also actively listening to your partner. Practice active listening by giving your full attention, maintaining eye contact, and validating your partner's feelings.

Healthy communication also includes resolving conflicts in a respectful and non-violent manner. Avoid resorting to manipulation, blame, or aggression. Rather, concentrate on working together to find solutions and making concessions when needed. Healthy communication is a two-way street, and both partners should feel comfortable expressing themselves.

Trust and Honesty

An essential component of a happy relationship is trust. It is gradually developed with constant integrity, dependability, and candid communication. Be transparent with your partner and avoid keeping secrets or hiding important information. Trust is fragile, so it is crucial to be trustworthy and to trust your partner as well.

Building trust also involves setting and respecting boundaries. Communicate your boundaries and expectations, and be respectful of your partner's boundaries as well. Trust is nurtured when both partners feel safe and respected within the relationship.

Equality and Mutual Respect

Mutual respect and equality are the cornerstones of healthy relationships. Each partner should be treated as an equal and have their opinions, feelings, and needs to be valued. Avoid any form of power imbalance or control within the relationship.

Respect is shown through kindness, empathy, and support. Celebrate each other's achievements, listen to each other's perspectives, and validate each other's emotions. Respect also means accepting each other's differences and allowing space for individual growth and self-expression.

Emotional Support and Empathy

In a healthy relationship, both partners should provide emotional support and empathy to one another. This involves being there for each other during difficult times, offering a listening ear, and validating each other's emotions. Show empathy by trying to understand your partner's perspective and offering comfort and reassurance.

It is important to note that healthy relationships do not rely on one person to meet all of the other's emotional needs. Each partner should have a support system outside of the relationship, including friends, family, or therapists. This ensures that both individuals have a balanced and healthy approach to emotional support.

Shared Values and Interests

Having shared values and interests can strengthen the bond in a healthy relationship. It provides a sense of connection and allows for shared experiences and activities. Take the time to explore each other's interests and find common ground. This can involve trying new hobbies together, engaging in shared goals, or simply spending quality time doing activities you both enjoy.

It is also important to maintain individuality within the relationship. Each partner should have their interests and personal goals. Encourage and support each other's individual growth and allow space for independence.

Healthy Conflict Resolution

Conflict is a natural part of any relationship, but it is how conflicts are resolved that determines the health of the relationship. In healthy relationships, conflicts are approached with respect, empathy, and a willingness to find a solution that benefits both partners.

When disagreements occur, stand back and evaluate the circumstances. Avoid reacting impulsively or resorting to aggressive behavior. Instead, communicate your feelings and needs calmly and listen to your partner's perspective. Look for compromises and solutions that respect both individuals' boundaries and values.

Continuous Growth and Nurturing the Relationship

Building a healthy relationship is an ongoing process that requires continuous effort and growth. It is important to nurture the relationship by regularly expressing love and appreciation, engaging in quality time together, and supporting each other's personal growth.

Keep the lines of communication open and regularly check in with each other about the state of the relationship. Be open to feedback and willing to make adjustments when necessary. Building a healthy relationship is a journey, and it requires both partners to be committed to growth and mutual happiness.

By focusing on self-reflection, effective communication, trust, equality, empathy, shared values, healthy conflict resolution, and continuous growth, you can build a healthy and fulfilling relationship after leaving an abusive one.

Finding Joy and Happiness

Finding joy and happiness after leaving an abusive relationship can be a challenging and transformative journey. It is important to remember that you deserve happiness and that it is possible to rebuild your life in a positive and fulfilling way.

Cultivating Self-Love and Self-Care

One of the first steps in finding joy and happiness is to cultivate self-love and prioritize self-care. After experiencing abuse, it is common to have low self-esteem and a negative self-image. However, by practicing self-love and self-care, you can begin to heal and rebuild your sense of self-worth.

Start by treating yourself with kindness and compassion. Engage in activities that bring you joy and make you feel good about yourself. This could include hobbies, exercise, spending time with loved ones, or engaging in self-care practices such as taking relaxing baths or practicing mindfulness.

You must look after your physical and emotional health. Make sure to prioritize your health by eating nutritious meals, getting enough sleep, and engaging in regular exercise. Consider seeking therapy or counseling to work through any lingering trauma and to develop healthy coping mechanisms.

Rediscovering Your Passions and Interests

Leaving an abusive relationship provides an opportunity to rediscover your passions and interests. During the relationship, you may have been discouraged or prevented from pursuing activities that brought you joy. Now is the time to reconnect with those interests and explore new ones.

Consider for a moment what makes you happy in the real world. It may be a good idea to reintegrate any past interests or pastimes you had before the abusive relationship. Whether it's painting, playing a musical instrument, gardening, or writing, engaging in activities that ignite your passion can bring a sense of fulfillment and joy.

Be open to trying new things. Explore different hobbies, join clubs or groups that align with your interests, or take classes to learn new skills. This can not only help you discover new sources of happiness but also provide opportunities to meet like-minded individuals and build new friendships.

Nurturing Supportive Relationships

Building healthy and supportive relationships is essential for finding joy and happiness. Surrounding yourself with people who uplift and support you can make a significant difference in your overall well-being.

Reach out to trusted friends and family members who have shown their support throughout your journey. Share your experiences and feelings with them, and allow them to be there for you. Building a strong support system can provide a sense of belonging, validation, and love.

Consider joining support groups or attending therapy sessions specifically designed for survivors of abuse. These spaces can offer a safe and understanding environment where you can connect with others who have had similar experiences. Sharing your stories, listening to others, and receiving support from individuals who truly understand can be incredibly empowering and healing.

Practicing Gratitude and Mindfulness

Practicing gratitude and mindfulness can help shift your focus towards the positive aspects of your life and cultivate a sense of joy and happiness. Recognizing and enjoying the positive aspects of your life, regardless of how minor they may seem, is the essence of gratitude.

Spend a few minutes every day thinking about the things you have to be thankful for. Simple things like a mouthwatering dinner, a thoughtful gesture from a buddy, or a stunning sunset could suffice. By consciously focusing on the positive aspects of your life, you can train your mind to notice and appreciate the joy that surrounds you.

Mindfulness, on the other hand, involves being fully present in the moment and non-judgmentally observing your thoughts and emotions. By practicing mindfulness, you can develop a greater sense of self-awareness and learn to let go of negative thoughts and emotions that may hinder your happiness.

Engage in mindfulness practices such as meditation, deep breathing exercises, or simply taking a few moments each day to tune into your senses and observe your surroundings. By cultivating a mindful mindset, you can find peace and joy in the present moment.

Setting Realistic Goals and Celebrating Achievements

Setting realistic goals and celebrating your achievements is an important part of finding joy and happiness. After leaving an abusive relationship, It is critical to concentrate on rebuilding your life and developing a future that is consistent with your values and aspirations.

Start by setting small, achievable goals that are meaningful to you. These goals could be related to your career, education, personal growth, or any other area of your life that you wish to improve. Break them down into smaller steps and celebrate each milestone along the way.

By setting and achieving goals, you can regain a sense of control and accomplishment. Your strength and tenacity are demonstrated by every stride you take ahead. Celebrate your achievements, no matter how small, and acknowledge the progress you have made. This will help boost your self-confidence and bring a sense of joy and fulfillment.

Embracing a Positive Mindset

Finding joy and happiness after leaving an abusive relationship requires embracing a positive mindset. It is important to let go of the past and focus on the present and future. While the healing process may take time, it is essential to believe in your ability to create a life filled with joy, love, and happiness.

Challenge negative thoughts and replace them with positive affirmations. Surround yourself with positive influences, whether it's through books, podcasts, or inspirational quotes. Practice self-compassion and remind yourself that you are deserving of happiness and love.

Finding joy and happiness is a personal journey, and it may look different for everyone. Be patient with yourself and allow yourself to experience a range of emotions as you navigate this new chapter of your life. With time, self-care, and a positive mindset, you can find joy and happiness beyond the chains of an abusive relationship.

Embracing Your Strength and Resilience

Recovering from an abusive relationship is a journey that requires immense strength and resilience. It is not an easy path, but it can lead to healing, growth, and a brighter future. In this section, we will explore how you can embrace your inner strength and resilience to move forward and create a life free from abuse.

Acknowledging Your Strength

One of the first steps in embracing your strength and resilience is acknowledging the courage it took to leave an abusive relationship. Leaving an abusive partner is a brave decision that requires immense strength and determination. By recognizing and acknowledging your strength, you can begin to build a solid foundation for your healing journey.

Think back for a moment on the difficulties you have successfully overcome. Remember the times when you stood up for yourself, set boundaries, or took steps towards leaving the abusive relationship. These moments are a testament to your strength and resilience. By acknowledging and celebrating these achievements, you can start to see yourself as the strong and capable person you truly are.

Cultivating Self-Compassion

Following an abusive relationship, it's normal to feel guilty, ashamed, and responsible for your actions. It is important to know that you are not to blame for the abuse you endured. Cultivating self-compassion is crucial in embracing your strength and resilience.

Practicing self-compassion entails being compassionate, understanding, and accepting of oneself. It means recognizing that you are human and that you deserve love, care, and support. Practice self-compassion by speaking to yourself with kindness, challenging negative self-talk, and engaging in activities that bring you joy and comfort.

Building a Support Network

Surrounding yourself with a strong support network is essential in embracing your strength and resilience. Reach out to friends, family members, or support groups who can provide you with the emotional support and encouragement you need. Sharing your experiences with others who have gone through similar situations can be incredibly empowering and validating.

Consider joining support groups or therapy sessions specifically designed for survivors of abuse. These spaces provide a safe and non-judgmental environment where you can share your story, gain insights, and learn coping strategies from others who have walked a similar path.

Practicing Self-Care

Self-care is a vital component of embracing your strength and resilience. It entails placing your physical, mental, and emotional well-being first. Engaging in self-care activities can help you reconnect with yourself, rebuild your self-esteem, and regain a sense of control over your life.

Explore different self-care practices that resonate with you. This could include activities such as exercise, meditation, journaling, spending time in nature, or pursuing hobbies and interests. Self-care is not selfish; it is a necessary part of your healing journey.

Setting Boundaries and Asserting Yourself

Embracing your strength and resilience also means learning to set boundaries and assert yourself in relationships. It's normal to battle with trust and fear of hurting again after being abused. By setting clear boundaries and communicating your needs, you can create healthier and more respectful relationships.

Practice assertiveness skills by expressing your thoughts, feelings, and boundaries calmly and assertively. Learn to say no when something does not align with your values or makes you uncomfortable. By setting and enforcing boundaries, you are reclaiming your power and ensuring that your needs are respected.

Celebrating Your Progress

Throughout your healing journey, it is important to celebrate your progress, no matter how small it may seem. Each step forward, no matter how tiny, is a testament to your strength and resilience. Take the time to acknowledge and celebrate your achievements, whether it is reaching a personal goal, overcoming a fear, or simply taking care of yourself.

By celebrating your progress, you are reinforcing your belief in your strength and resilience. It serves as a reminder that you have the power to create a life free from abuse and to build healthy and fulfilling relationships.

Seeking Professional Help

While embracing your strength and resilience is a significant part of your healing journey, it is important to recognize that professional help can also be beneficial. Therapists, counselors, and support groups specialized in trauma and abuse can provide you with the guidance, tools, and support you need to navigate the challenges you may face.

Professional help can assist you in processing your emotions, healing from trauma, and developing healthy coping mechanisms. It can also provide you with a safe space to explore your experiences, gain insights, and work towards building a brighter future.

Embracing your strength and resilience is a continuous process. It takes time, patience, and self-compassion. Be gentle with yourself as you navigate this journey and trust that you have the inner strength to create a life filled with love, happiness, and freedom.

Chapter 7: Supporting Others

Recognizing Signs in Others

When it comes to recognizing signs of abuse in others, it is important to be observant and aware of the warning signs. There are many different types of abuse, such as verbal, physical, emotional, sexual, and financial abuse. It can occur in any type of relationship, whether it be romantic, familial, or even friendship. By understanding the signs, we can better support and help those who may be experiencing abuse.

Physical Signs

Although there are some common symptoms to watch out for, physical evidence of abuse may not always be evident. These can include unexplained injuries such as bruises, cuts, or burns, especially if they appear in patterns or are recurring. The person may also try to hide these injuries by wearing clothing that covers them, even in inappropriate situations. They may have frequent visits to the emergency room or doctor with vague explanations for their injuries.

Emotional and Behavioral Signs

Not only can emotional abuse do harm, but it can also be more difficult to identify than physical violence. Some emotional and behavioral signs to watch for include:

Low self-esteem: The person may constantly put themselves down, have a negative self-image, or express feelings of worthlessness.

Withdrawal from activities and relationships: They may isolate themselves from friends and family, avoid social situations, or make excuses for not participating in activities they once enjoyed.

Personality changes: They may become more anxious, depressed, or irritable. They may also exhibit signs of fear or paranoia.

Unexplained changes in behavior: They may start engaging in self-destructive behaviors such as substance abuse or self-harm.

Constantly seeking approval: They may constantly seek validation and approval from others, often apologizing excessively or feeling guilty for things that are not their fault.

Verbal and Psychological Signs

Verbal and psychological abuse can be just as damaging as physical abuse, if not more so. Among the warning indicators are:

Constant criticism and belittling: The person may be subjected to constant criticism, insults, and put-downs, which can erode their self-esteem and self-worth.

Gaslighting: The abuser may manipulate the person's perception of reality, making them doubt their memory, perception, and sanity.

Controlling behavior: The abuser may exert control over every aspect of the person's life, including their finances, social interactions, and daily activities.

Threats and intimidation: The person may be subjected to threats of violence, harm to loved ones, or other forms of intimidation to maintain control.

Isolation: The abuser may isolate the person from friends and family, making them dependent on the abuser for support and companionship.

Signs of Sexual Abuse

Sexual abuse is a deeply traumatic experience, and it is important to be aware of the signs. Some indicators of sexual abuse include:

Unexplained physical injuries: The person may have unexplained injuries to their genital area, bruises, or other signs of trauma.

Changes in behavior: They may exhibit sudden changes in behavior, such as becoming withdrawn, anxious, or displaying signs of depression.

Sexualized behavior: They may display sexualized behavior that is inappropriate for their age or developmental stage.

Fear or avoidance of certain people or places: They may exhibit fear or avoidance of specific individuals or places associated with the abuse.

Difficulty in forming healthy relationships: They may struggle with forming and maintaining healthy relationships, often experiencing trust issues and difficulties with intimacy.

Financial Abuse

Financial abuse is a form of control where the abuser exerts power over the person's finances. Signs of financial abuse may include:

Limited access to money: All financial decisions may be controlled by the abuser, and the victim may only have restricted access to their funds.

Forced dependence: The abuser may prevent the person from working or accessing education, making them financially dependent on the abuser.

Monitoring and controlling spending: The abuser may closely monitor and control every aspect of the person's spending, often restricting access to necessities.

Identity theft: The abuser may use the person's personal information without their consent, opening accounts or taking out loans in their name.

Trusting Your Instincts

It is important to trust your instincts when it comes to recognizing signs of abuse in others. If something feels off or you suspect someone may be experiencing abuse, it is crucial to approach the situation with empathy and support. Anybody, regardless of age, gender, or background, can become the victim of abuse. By being aware of the signs and offering support, you can help break the chains of abuse and provide a safe space for those who need it.

Offering Support and Resources

Supporting someone who is in an abusive relationship can be challenging, but it is crucial to provide them with the help and resources they need to break free from the cycle of abuse. On their path to recovery and healing, your assistance can have a big impact.

Listen without judgment

One of the most important things you can do when offering support to someone in an abusive relationship is to listen to them without judgment. Create a safe and non-judgmental space where they can openly share their experiences, fears, and concerns. It is essential to validate their feelings and let them know that you believe and support them. Avoid blaming or criticizing them for their choices or actions, as this can further isolate them and make it harder for them to seek help.

Educate yourself

You must educate yourself about the nature of abuse and the tools available to support someone in an abusive relationship. Learn about the different forms of abuse, such as physical, emotional, verbal, and financial abuse. Understand the cycle of abuse and the tactics used by abusers to maintain control over their victims. By educating yourself, you will be better equipped to provide informed support and guidance.

Offer Resources and Information

Provide the person with information about local resources and support services available to them. This can include helplines, shelters, counseling services, legal aid, and support groups. Research and compile a list of these resources, including their contact information and any relevant details. Offer to accompany them to appointments or help them make phone calls if they feel comfortable with it. Give them the respect they deserve and let them decide for themselves.

Safety planning

Putting safety plans in place is essential to helping someone who is in an abusive relationship. Help them create a safety plan that outlines steps they can take to protect themselves and their children, if applicable. This plan may include identifying safe places to go, developing a code word or signal to communicate distress, and gathering important documents and belongings in a safe location. Encourage them to practice self-care and develop a support network of trusted friends or family members who can assist them during difficult times.

Encourage professional help

Encourage the person to seek professional help from therapists, counselors, or support groups specializing in domestic violence. Professional intervention can provide them with the necessary tools and guidance to heal from the trauma and rebuild their lives. Offer to help them research and find reputable professionals in their area. If they are hesitant or resistant to seeking professional help, remind them that they deserve to live a life free from abuse and that seeking support is a sign of strength.

Be patient and understanding

The process of getting over an abusive relationship is difficult and complex. It is essential to be patient and understanding with the person as they navigate their way toward healing and recovery. They may experience setbacks, doubts, and conflicting emotions along the way. Offer them your support and reassurance, reminding them that they are not alone and that you are there for them. Avoid pressuring them to make decisions or take actions they are not ready for, as this can further undermine their sense of control.

Maintain confidentiality

Respect the person's privacy and maintain confidentiality. It is crucial not to share their experiences or personal information without their explicit consent. Confidentiality is essential in building trust and ensuring their safety. If you are concerned about their immediate safety, consult with professionals or helplines to determine the best course of action while still respecting their privacy.

Take care of yourself

It can be extremely taxing and difficult to support someone who is in an abusive relationship. It is essential to prioritize your well-being and seek support for yourself as well. To share your feelings and experiences, get in touch with loved ones, friends, or support groups. Practice self-care activities that help you relax and recharge.

Promote community awareness

Advocate for community awareness and education about domestic violence. Encourage discussions and workshops in schools, workplaces, and community centers to raise awareness about the signs of abuse and the resources available. By promoting awareness, you can help break the silence surrounding domestic violence and empower others to seek help and support.

Offer ongoing support

It takes more than one instance to support someone who is in an abusive relationship. It requires ongoing support and understanding. Check in with the person regularly, offering a listening ear and reassurance. Let them know that you are there for them, even after they have left the abusive relationship. Be patient and understanding as they continue their healing journey, and celebrate their progress and achievements along the way.

Offering support to someone in an abusive relationship can be challenging, but your presence and support can make a significant difference in their life. By providing them with resources, understanding, and non-judgmental space, you can help them break free from the chains of abuse and embark on a journey toward healing, empowerment, and a life free from violence.

Understanding Boundaries in Helping

When it comes to supporting others who are in abusive relationships, it is crucial to understand and respect boundaries. Boundaries play a significant role in maintaining healthy relationships and ensuring the well-being of both the helper and the person being helped.

The Importance of Boundaries

Boundaries are essential in any relationship, including the helping relationship. They establish the bounds of what is reasonable and comfortable for each party. In the context of supporting someone in an abusive relationship, boundaries help establish a framework for assisting while maintaining personal well-being and preventing burnout.

By setting clear boundaries, you can ensure that you are providing support in a way that is sustainable and healthy for both parties. Boundaries also help maintain a sense of autonomy and respect for the person you are helping, allowing them to make their own decisions and take control of their situation.

Establishing Boundaries

Establishing boundaries begins with self-reflection and understanding your limitations, needs, and values. It is important to recognize that you cannot be everything to everyone and that it is okay to prioritize your well-being. Take the time to identify what you are comfortable with and what you are not comfortable with in terms of the support you can provide.

Once you have a clear understanding of your boundaries, communicate them openly and honestly with the person you are helping. Let them know what you are willing and able to do and what you are not. This openness will aid in controlling expectations and avert misconceptions.

Respecting Boundaries

Respecting boundaries is just as important as establishing them. It is crucial to honor the boundaries set by the person you are helping, even if you disagree or feel that they are making choices that may not be in their best interest. Everyone has the right to make their own decisions, even if they believe they are not the right ones.

Respecting boundaries also means not overstepping or trying to control the person's actions or decisions. It is essential to provide support without taking away their agency or autonomy. Instead, focus on empowering them to make informed choices and offering resources and information that can help them make decisions that align with their goals and values.

Challenges in Maintaining Boundaries

Maintaining boundaries in helping relationships can be challenging, especially when dealing with sensitive and emotionally charged situations like abusive relationships. It is common to feel a strong desire to protect and rescue the person from their situation, but it is important to know that you cannot fix or save them.

One of the challenges is managing your own emotions and reactions. It is natural to feel anger, frustration, or sadness when hearing about the abuse someone is experiencing. It is crucial to process these emotions healthily and not let them interfere with your ability to provide support.

Another challenge is dealing with resistance or pushback from the person you are helping. They may not be ready or willing to accept the support you are offering, or they may have different expectations of what help should look like. In these situations, it is important to respect their boundaries and be patient. Offer support without imposing your agenda or forcing them to make decisions they are not ready for.

Self-Care and Boundaries

Maintaining healthy boundaries in helping relationships also requires taking care of yourself. It can be extremely taxing to support someone in an abusive relationship, and it may bring up memories of trauma or events from the past. It is crucial to prioritize self-care and seek support for yourself when needed.

Make time for the things that will help you feel refreshed and renewed. Practice self-compassion and engage in activities that promote your well-being. You cannot pour from an empty cup, and taking care of yourself allows you to show up as a more effective and supportive helper.

Seeking Supervision and Support

If you find yourself struggling to maintain boundaries or feeling overwhelmed by the helping process, it is important to seek supervision and support. Consult with a supervisor, mentor, or therapist who can provide guidance and help you navigate the challenges that may arise.

Supervision can offer a space to reflect on your experiences, process your emotions, and gain insights into your reactions and triggers. It can also provide an opportunity to learn from others' experiences and receive guidance on how to navigate complex situations.

Understanding and respecting boundaries in helping relationships is crucial when supporting someone in an abusive relationship. By establishing and communicating boundaries effectively, you can provide support in a way that is sustainable and healthy for both parties. Prioritize self-care and seek support when needed. By maintaining healthy boundaries, you can be a valuable source of support while also protecting your well-being.

Promoting Awareness and Advocacy

Promoting awareness and advocacy is crucial in addressing the issue of abusive relationships and working towards creating a safer and more supportive society. By raising awareness about the signs of abuse, the impact it has on individuals and communities, and the resources available for support, we can empower individuals to recognize and address abusive behaviors. Advocacy plays a vital role in supporting survivors, challenging societal norms, and promoting systemic change to prevent abuse in the future.

Understanding the Importance of Awareness

Awareness is the first step towards addressing any issue, and it is no different when it comes to abusive relationships. Many individuals may not even realize that they are in an abusive relationship or may be unsure about the signs and dynamics of abuse. By promoting awareness, we can help individuals recognize the signs of abuse, understand the impact it has on their well-being, and encourage them to seek help.

Raising awareness also helps to break the silence and stigma surrounding abusive relationships. By openly discussing the issue, we can create a safe space for survivors to share their experiences, seek support, and break free from the cycle of abuse. It also sends a powerful message to abusers that their behavior will not be tolerated and that society stands united against all forms of abuse.

Educating the Community

Education is a key component of promoting awareness and advocacy. By providing accurate and comprehensive information about abusive relationships, we can equip individuals with the knowledge they need to recognize and respond to abuse effectively. This education should be targeted at various levels, including schools, workplaces, community organizations, and religious institutions.

In schools, it is essential to incorporate age-appropriate education about healthy relationships, consent, and boundaries. By teaching young people about healthy relationship dynamics and the warning signs of abuse, we can empower them to make informed choices and develop respectful behaviors.

Workplaces can also play a significant role in promoting awareness. Employers can provide training sessions on recognizing and addressing abuse, as well as creating policies that support employees who may be experiencing abuse. By fostering a supportive and understanding environment, workplaces can become a haven for survivors and encourage them to seek help.

Community organizations and religious institutions can organize workshops, seminars, and awareness campaigns to educate their members about abusive relationships. By engaging with the community, these organizations can provide resources, support, and a network of individuals who are committed to ending abuse.

Collaborating with Support Services

Promoting awareness and advocacy requires collaboration with support services that specialize in assisting survivors of abuse. These organizations play a crucial role in providing resources, counseling, and shelter to those in need. By partnering with them, we can ensure that survivors have access to the support they require and that their voices are heard.

Collaboration can take various forms, including fundraising events, awareness campaigns, and joint initiatives. Together, we can increase our impact and connect with more people. It is essential to establish strong relationships with support services to ensure a coordinated and effective response to the issue of abusive relationships.

Challenging Societal Norms

Advocacy goes beyond raising awareness; it involves challenging societal norms and attitudes that perpetuate abuse. Many cultural, social, and gender norms contribute to the prevalence of abusive relationships. By challenging these norms, we can create a culture that promotes equality, respect, and non-violence.

Advocacy efforts should focus on promoting gender equality, consent, and healthy relationship dynamics. This can be achieved through public campaigns, media engagement, and community dialogues. By highlighting positive role models, sharing survivor stories, and showcasing healthy relationship behaviors, we can shift societal attitudes and beliefs.

Engaging Policy Makers

Advocacy also involves engaging policymakers to create systemic change. Laws and policies play a crucial role in addressing abusive relationships and protecting survivors. By advocating for legislation that supports survivors, holds abusers accountable, and promotes prevention, we can create a legal framework that prioritizes the safety and well-being of individuals.

Engaging policymakers can include lobbying for changes in existing laws, advocating for increased funding for support services, and pushing for educational reforms. By working with lawmakers, we can ensure that the issue of abusive relationships remains a priority on the political agenda and that survivors' voices are heard.

Supporting Research and Data Collection

Advocacy efforts should also focus on supporting research and data collection to better understand the prevalence and impact of abusive relationships. By collecting accurate and comprehensive data, we can identify trends, gaps in services, and areas that require further attention. This information is crucial in shaping effective policies, programs, and interventions.

Supporting research can involve funding studies, participating in surveys, and collaborating with academic institutions. By promoting research, we can contribute to the body of knowledge on abusive relationships and ensure that evidence-based practices are implemented.

Empowering Individuals to Advocate

Lastly, promoting awareness and advocacy involves empowering individuals to become advocates themselves. By providing training, resources, and support, we can encourage survivors, allies, and community members to speak out against abuse and work towards creating a safer society.

Empowering individuals to advocate can include providing public speaking opportunities, organizing workshops on advocacy skills, and creating platforms for survivors to share their stories. By amplifying their voices and experiences, we can inspire others to take action and join the movement against abusive relationships.

Promoting awareness and advocacy is essential in addressing the issue of abusive relationships. By raising awareness, educating the community, collaborating with support services, challenging societal norms, engaging policymakers, supporting research, and empowering individuals to advocate, we can create a society that prioritizes safety, respect, and equality. Together, we can break the chains of abuse and build a future free from violence.

Chapter 8: Breaking the Cycle

Preventing Abuse in Future Relationships

Preventing abuse in future relationships is crucial for breaking the cycle of violence and creating a healthier and safer environment for ourselves and those around us. It requires a deep understanding of the dynamics of abuse, as well as a commitment to personal growth and self-awareness.

Understanding the Dynamics of Abuse

To prevent abuse in future relationships, it is essential to understand the dynamics of abuse and the warning signs that may indicate a potentially abusive partner. There are many different types of abuse, such as verbal, physical, emotional, sexual, and financial abuse. It usually begins quietly and builds up gradually over time.

One of the most important steps in preventing abuse is recognizing the red flags early on. These may include controlling behaviors, possessiveness, jealousy, disrespect, manipulation, and a lack of empathy. It is crucial to trust your instincts and not dismiss any concerns or doubts you may have about a potential partner's behavior.

Building Healthy Communication Skills

A strong relationship is built on effective communication. By developing strong communication skills, we can prevent misunderstandings, resolve conflicts peacefully, and foster mutual respect and understanding. Here are some key principles to keep in mind:

Active Listening: Practice active listening by giving your full attention to your partner, maintaining eye contact, and validating their feelings and experiences. Avoid interrupting or dismissing their concerns.

Expressing Emotions: Learn to express your emotions healthily and constructively. Use "I" statements to communicate your feelings and needs without blaming or attacking your partner.

Setting Boundaries: Establish clear boundaries and communicate them openly with your partner. Recognize each other's limits and be prepared to make concessions when needed.

Conflict Resolution: Develop effective conflict resolution skills by focusing on finding solutions rather than winning arguments. Practice empathy, compromise, and finding common ground.

Cultivating Equality and Respect

Preventing abuse in future relationships requires cultivating a culture of equality and respect. It is essential to recognize that all individuals deserve to be treated with dignity and respect, regardless of their gender, race, or any other characteristic. Here are some ways to promote equality and respect in your relationships:

Mutual Consent: Prioritize mutual consent in all aspects of your relationship, including physical intimacy. Both partners should feel comfortable and empowered to express their boundaries and desires.

Shared Decision-Making: Make decisions together and value each other's opinions and perspectives. Avoid controlling or dominating behaviors that undermine the autonomy of your partner.

Equal Power Dynamics: Strive for equal power dynamics in your relationship. Avoid power imbalances and ensure that both partners have an equal say in important decisions.

Challenging Gender Stereotypes: Challenge traditional gender roles and stereotypes that perpetuate inequality and reinforce harmful behaviors. Promote candid conversations around gender norms and expectations.

Promoting Healthy Conflict Resolution

Conflict is a natural part of any relationship, but it is how we handle conflicts that can make a significant difference. By promoting healthy conflict resolution, we can prevent the escalation of disagreements into abusive behaviors. Here are some strategies to promote healthy conflict resolution:

Calm Communication: Maintain a calm and respectful tone during conflicts. Avoid yelling, name-calling, or using derogatory language.

Active Problem-Solving: Focus on finding solutions rather than blaming each other. Collaborate and brainstorm together to find mutually beneficial resolutions.

Taking Responsibility: Take responsibility for your actions and apologize when necessary. Avoid defensiveness and be open to feedback and constructive criticism.

Seeking Mediation: If conflicts become challenging to resolve, consider seeking the help of a neutral third party, such as a therapist or counselor, to facilitate healthy communication and conflict resolution.

Promoting Emotional Intelligence

Emotional intelligence plays a vital role in preventing abuse in future relationships. By developing emotional intelligence, we can better understand and manage our emotions, as well as empathize with and support our partners. Here are a few strategies for developing emotional intelligence:

Self-Awareness: Cultivate self-awareness by reflecting on your emotions, triggers, and patterns of behavior. Understand how your emotions can impact your interactions with others.

Empathy: Practice empathy by putting yourself in your partner's shoes and trying to understand their perspective. Acknowledge their feelings and express sincere concern and caring.

Emotional Regulation: Learn healthy ways to manage and regulate your emotions. Avoid lashing out or using emotional manipulation as a means of control.

Emotional Support: Offer emotional support to your partner by being a good listener, providing comfort, and offering encouragement. Provide a judgment-free environment where they feel free to express their emotions.

By implementing these strategies and principles, we can actively work towards preventing abuse in future relationships. Building healthy relationships is an ongoing process that requires continuous effort, self-reflection, and open communication. Together, we can break the cycle of abuse and create a world where respect, equality, and love thrive.

Teaching Healthy Relationship Skills

To break the cycle of abuse and promote healthy relationships, it is crucial to educate individuals on the skills needed to establish and maintain healthy connections with others. Teaching healthy relationship skills not only empowers individuals to build strong and respectful partnerships but also helps prevent future instances of abuse.

Communication and Active Listening

Good communication is one of the key pillars of a happy relationship. Teaching individuals how to express their thoughts, feelings, and needs respectfully and assertively is essential. Encouraging open and honest communication helps create an environment where both partners feel heard and understood.

Active listening is another crucial skill that should be emphasized. It involves giving full attention to the speaker, maintaining eye contact, and providing verbal and non-verbal cues to show understanding and empathy. By teaching active listening, individuals can develop stronger connections and foster mutual understanding within their relationships.

Conflict Resolution

Conflict is a natural part of any relationship, but it is how conflicts are resolved that determines the health of the partnership. Teaching healthy conflict resolution skills equips individuals with the tools to address disagreements in a constructive and non-violent manner.

Encouraging individuals to approach conflicts with empathy, understanding, and a willingness to find a compromise can help prevent the escalation of disagreements into abusive situations. Teaching techniques such as active problem-solving, negotiation, and finding win-win solutions can empower individuals to resolve conflicts in a way that strengthens their relationship rather than causing harm.

Boundaries and Consent

Understanding and respecting personal boundaries is crucial in any healthy relationship. Teaching individuals about the importance of setting and communicating their boundaries helps establish a foundation of respect and consent. It is essential to emphasize that boundaries should be mutually agreed upon and can be renegotiated as the relationship evolves.

Teaching about consent is also vital in preventing abusive behavior. Individuals should be educated on the importance of obtaining clear and enthusiastic consent in all aspects of a relationship, including physical intimacy. By promoting a culture of consent, we can create an environment where all individuals feel safe, respected, and in control of their bodies.

Emotional Intelligence and Empathy

Developing emotional intelligence and empathy is key to fostering healthy relationships. Teaching individuals to recognize and understand their own emotions, as well as the emotions of their partner, can help prevent misunderstandings and promote empathy.

By encouraging individuals to practice empathy, they can better understand their partner's perspective, validate their feelings, and respond with compassion. Emotional intelligence also involves managing and expressing emotions in a healthy and non-destructive way, which is crucial in maintaining a respectful and supportive relationship.

Equality and Respect

Promoting gender equality and respect is essential in teaching healthy relationship skills. Individuals should be educated on the importance of treating their partners as equals and valuing their opinions, desires, and autonomy. By challenging traditional gender roles and stereotypes, we can create a culture that values and respects all individuals, regardless of their gender.

Teaching about respect goes beyond gender equality and extends to all aspects of a relationship. Individuals should be encouraged to respect each other's boundaries, opinions, and personal space. By fostering a culture of respect, we can prevent power imbalances and create relationships based on mutual trust and equality.

Healthy Role Models and Media Literacy

Exposing individuals to healthy relationship role models and promoting media literacy can greatly contribute to teaching healthy relationship skills. By highlighting positive examples of healthy relationships in various forms of media, individuals can learn what healthy dynamics look like and aspire to emulate them.

Teaching media literacy helps individuals critically analyze and challenge unhealthy relationship portrayals in the media. By understanding the influence of media on our perceptions of relationships, individuals can develop a more realistic and healthy understanding of what constitutes a respectful and loving partnership.

Education and Prevention Programs

To effectively teach healthy relationship skills, it is crucial to implement comprehensive education and prevention programs. These programs should be integrated into school curricula, community centers, and other relevant settings. By providing individuals with the knowledge and skills needed to establish and maintain healthy relationships, we can prevent future instances of abuse and promote a culture of respect and equality.

Education and prevention programs should cover topics such as communication, conflict resolution, consent, boundaries, emotional intelligence, and respect. These programs should be age-appropriate and tailored to the specific needs of different populations, including adolescents, young adults, and adults.

By investing in teaching healthy relationship skills, we can empower individuals to break the cycle of abuse, build strong and respectful partnerships, and contribute to creating a society that values and promotes healthy relationships for all.

Promoting Gender Equality and Respect

Gender equality and respect are fundamental principles that should be promoted in all aspects of society, including relationships. To break the cycle of abuse, it is crucial to address the underlying issues of power imbalances and societal norms that perpetuate harmful behaviors.

Understanding Gender Equality

The term "gender equality" describes how people of all genders should be treated equally and have equal access to opportunities. It recognizes that both men and women should have the same access to resources, decision-making power, and social, economic, and political opportunities. In the context of relationships, gender equality means that both partners have an equal say in decision-making, share responsibilities, and respect each other's autonomy and boundaries.

Challenging Gender Stereotypes

One of the key factors that contribute to the perpetuation of abusive behaviors is the presence of rigid gender stereotypes. These stereotypes dictate how individuals should behave based on their gender, reinforcing power imbalances and unequal dynamics in relationships. To promote gender equality and respect, it is essential to challenge and break down these stereotypes.

Encouraging open discussions about gender roles and expectations can help individuals recognize and question the harmful effects of these stereotypes. By promoting the idea that both men and women can engage in any activity or pursue any career they desire, we can create a more inclusive and equal society. It is important to teach children from a young age that their worth is not determined by their gender, and that they should be free to express themselves authentically.

Communication and Active Listening

Effective communication is a cornerstone of healthy relationships. It involves actively listening to your partner, expressing your thoughts and feelings honestly and respectfully, and working together to find mutually beneficial solutions. By promoting open and honest communication, we can create an environment where both partners feel heard, valued, and respected.

Active listening involves giving your full attention to your partner, without interrupting or judging. It requires empathy and understanding, as well as the willingness to validate your partner's experiences and emotions. By practicing active listening, we can foster a sense of trust and emotional intimacy in our relationships.

Mutual Respect and Consent

A vital component of any happy relationship is respect. It involves recognizing and valuing your partner's autonomy, boundaries, and opinions. In a relationship based on mutual respect, both partners feel safe and supported to express themselves without fear of judgment or retribution.

Consent is another crucial element of respectful relationships. It means that both partners freely and willingly agree to engage in any sexual activity. Consent ought to be passionate, ongoing, and founded on unambiguous communication. It is important to recollect that consent can be withdrawn at any time, and that coercion or pressure should never be used to obtain it.

Sharing Responsibilities

To promote gender equality, it is important to share responsibilities and decision-making in relationships. This means that both partners contribute equally to household chores, childcare, and financial decisions. By sharing responsibilities, we can challenge traditional gender roles and create a more balanced and equitable dynamic.

It is important to have open discussions about expectations and responsibilities early on in a relationship. By setting clear boundaries and establishing shared goals, both partners can work together to create a partnership based on equality and respect.

Education and Awareness

Promoting gender equality and respect requires ongoing education and awareness. It is important to stay informed about the issues surrounding gender inequality and to actively challenge discriminatory attitudes and behaviors. This can be done through reading books and articles, attending workshops and seminars, and engaging in conversations with others.

Educational programs that focus on healthy relationships, consent, and gender equality can also play a crucial role in promoting positive change. By teaching young people about healthy relationship dynamics and the importance of respect, we can help prevent future instances of abuse.

Advocacy and Support

Promoting gender equality and respect also involves advocating for change at a societal level. This can be done by supporting organizations and initiatives that work towards gender equality, volunteering your time, or participating in advocacy campaigns. By raising awareness and challenging societal norms, we can create a culture that values and respects all individuals, regardless of their gender.

Supporting survivors of abuse is also an important aspect of promoting gender equality and respect. By providing a safe and non-judgmental space for survivors to share their experiences, we can help break the silence surrounding abuse and encourage others to seek help.

Promoting gender equality and respect is essential in breaking the cycle of abuse. By challenging gender stereotypes, fostering open communication, practicing mutual respect and consent, sharing responsibilities, and advocating for change, we can create healthier and more equitable relationships. It is through these efforts that we can build a society that values and respects all individuals, regardless of their gender.

Creating a Culture of Non-Violence

Creating a culture of non-violence is essential in breaking the cycle of abuse and promoting healthy relationships. It requires a collective effort from individuals, communities, and society as a whole. By addressing the root causes of violence and promoting respect, equality, and empathy, we can work towards building a safer and more peaceful world.

Understanding the Impact of Violence

Violence, in any form, has a profound impact on individuals and communities. It not only causes physical harm but also leaves deep emotional scars that can last a lifetime. The effects of violence can be seen in various aspects of a person's life, including their mental health, relationships, and overall well-being. By understanding the devastating consequences of violence, we can begin to recognize the urgency of creating a culture of non-violence.

Education and Awareness

One of the key steps in creating a culture of non-violence is education and awareness. It is crucial to educate individuals, especially young people, about healthy relationships, consent, and the importance of respect. By providing comprehensive education on these topics, we can empower individuals to recognize and reject abusive behaviors. Schools, community organizations, and families all play a vital role in promoting this education and raising awareness about the impact of violence.

Challenging Gender Stereotypes

Gender stereotypes and inequality contribute to the perpetuation of violence. It is essential to challenge these stereotypes and promote gender equality in all aspects of life. By dismantling harmful gender norms and promoting equal opportunities for all genders, we can create a society that values and respects everyone. This includes challenging traditional gender roles, promoting equal pay, and supporting women's empowerment. By addressing these issues, we can create a culture that rejects violence and promotes equality.

Teaching Conflict Resolution Skills

Conflict is a natural part of any relationship, but it is essential to teach individuals healthy ways to resolve conflicts without resorting to violence. By promoting effective communication, active listening, and empathy, we can equip individuals with the skills they need to navigate disagreements in a non-violent manner. Teaching conflict resolution skills from an early age can help break the cycle of violence and promote healthier relationships.

Promoting Emotional Intelligence

Emotional intelligence plays a crucial role in creating a culture of non-violence. By promoting emotional awareness, empathy, and self-regulation, we can help individuals develop healthier ways of expressing their emotions. This includes teaching individuals to recognize and manage anger, frustration, and other intense emotions in a non-violent manner. By fostering emotional intelligence, we can create a society that values emotional well-being and rejects violence as a means of expression.

Holding Perpetrators Accountable

Creating a culture of non-violence also requires holding perpetrators accountable for their actions. This includes implementing and enforcing laws that protect victims of violence and punish those who perpetrate it. It also involves providing support and resources for survivors to seek justice and heal from their experiences. By holding perpetrators accountable, we send a clear message that violence will not be tolerated in our society.

Supporting Survivors

Supporting survivors of violence is crucial in creating a culture of non-violence. It is essential to provide survivors with the necessary resources, such as counseling, support groups, and legal assistance, to help them heal and rebuild their lives. By offering a safe and supportive environment, we can empower survivors to break free from the cycle of abuse and create a future free from violence.

Engaging Men and Boys

Engaging men and boys in the conversation about violence prevention is vital. By challenging toxic masculinity and promoting healthy masculinity, we can create a culture that rejects violence and respects all genders. Engaging men and boys in discussions about consent, respect, and healthy relationships can help break down harmful stereotypes and promote positive change.

Advocacy and Policy Change

Creating a culture of non-violence also requires advocacy and policy change at the societal level. It is essential to advocate for policies that protect victims of violence, promote gender equality, and provide resources for prevention and intervention programs. By working together to change societal norms and attitudes towards violence, we can create a culture that values peace, respect, and equality.

Building Strong Communities

Building strong communities is crucial in creating a culture of non-violence. By fostering a sense of belonging, connection, and support, we can create environments where violence is less likely to occur.

This includes promoting community programs, support networks, and initiatives that bring people together and promote positive relationships. By building strong communities, we can create a collective commitment to non-violence and support those affected by abuse.

Creating a culture of non-violence is a long-term and ongoing process that requires the commitment and effort of individuals, communities, and society as a whole. By addressing the root causes of violence, promoting education and awareness, challenging harmful stereotypes, and supporting survivors, we can work towards a future where violence is no longer tolerated. Together, we can break the cycle of abuse and create a world built on respect, equality, and non-violence.

Conclusion

In the journey of breaking the chains of abusive relationships, we have delved deep into the dark corners of this pervasive issue. We have explored the different forms of abuse, recognized the signs, and understood the impact it has on its victims. But most importantly, we have discovered the power within us to break free and rebuild our lives.

Breaking free from the hold of an abusive relationship is no simple task. It requires immense courage, strength, and determination. It starts with acknowledging the abuse and its consequences, and gradually finding the inner strength to decide to leave. With the support of trusted friends, family, and professionals, we can develop an exit plan and secure the legal protection we need.

Yet, leaving is just the beginning of the healing process. Recovering from abuse takes time and patience. It involves prioritizing self-care and seeking professional help. Through therapy, counseling, and support groups, we can navigate the complex emotions and scars left behind by the abuse. We learn to rebuild our self-esteem, set boundaries, and establish healthier relationships.

Breaking the cycle of abuse also means equipping ourselves with knowledge and skills to prevent it in future relationships. We become vigilant in recognizing red flags and warning signs in potential partners. We prioritize healthy communication, conflict resolution, and mutual respect. We understand the importance of consent, personal boundaries, and equality. By doing so, we create a foundation for healthier, happier relationships.

As survivors, we have a responsibility to support one another and create a culture of empathy and understanding. By educating others about abusive relationships and breaking the stigma surrounding victims, we can pave the way for change. We provide resources, referrals, and support to organizations dedicated to assisting survivors. We become advocates for policy changes and legal protections. Through open dialogue and empathy, we foster a supportive community that stands against abuse.

In concluding this book, Breaking the Chains of Abusive Relationships, I want to emphasize that the journey of breaking free is not without its challenges. But it is a journey worth embarking on. It's a path of healing, empowerment, and self-discovery. It is a journey that leads to a brighter future.

To all those who have experienced the pain and torment of abuse, know that you are not alone. There is hope, there is support, and there is a life beyond the chains that once bound you. You have the strength within you to break free and embrace a future filled with love, respect, and happiness.

www.ingramcontent.com/pod-product-compliance
Lightning Source LLC
Chambersburg PA
CBHW070827250726
48662CB00003B/1110